MW00915246

OASIS

Ninja

A Home Health Nurse's Guide to Visits, Documentation, and Positive Patient Outcomes

Mark Aquino
RN MHA

Acknowledgements: Thank you to my wife Diane for always supporting me. Thank you also to all my family, teachers, and home health agencies that acted as my counselors and consultants. And thank you to our baby girl Kristel Candace for being our bundle of joy.

Table of Contents

Table of Contents	**4**
Preface	8
About the Author	9
Recommended Further Reading	10
Check out more books by the author at OASISNinja.com	10
Leave a Review!	10
SECTION 1 - Fundamentals	**12**
The Basics	**12**
Chapter 1 - Introduction - What is OASIS	**13**
Chapter 2 - What is Home Health Care?	**17**
Chapter 3 - What Makes a Great Home Health Nurse?	**22**
Chapter 4 - Home Health and CMS (Centers for Medicare & Medicaid Services)	**29**
Chapter 5 - Changes to OASIS E-1 Documentation	**32**
Chapter 6 - What is OASIS E-1?	**38**
Chapter 7 - New OASIS Items and Retired Items	**44**
Chapter 8 - The SOC Checklist in SOAP Format	**50**
Comprehensive SOC Checklist:	51
Simple Checklist:	54
Where to Download	56
Chapter 9 - What is a SOAP NOTE - SOAP Notes for Physical Assessment	**57**
SECTION 2 –	**62**
Before the Visit	**62**
Preparing to deal with people well in the home	**62**
Chapter 10 - The Three Phases of the Nurse-Client Relationship	**63**
Chapter 11 - Therapeutic Communication - Improving Therapeutic Communication	**70**
Chapter 12 - Importance of Active Listening	**79**

Chapter 13 - How to Use Silence Effectively - Intentional Silence   **84**

Chapter 14 - Nontherapeutic Communication - What to Avoid **89**

Chapter 15 - Stress Management for Nurses   **94**

Chapter 16 - Time Management For Nurses - Effective Use of Time   **102**

    How Time Management Can Help You Get More Done in Less Time   **102**

Chapter 17 - Improving Your Emotional Self-Regulation   **107**

Chapter 18 - How to Read a History and Physical Examination (H&P)   **110**

Chapter 19 - Pathophysiology - Importance in Home Health **113**

    CARDIAC: 114

    DERMATOLOGY: 114

    EARS, EYES, NOSE, THROAT (EENT):   115

    ENDOCRINE AND METABOLIC: 116

    GASTROINTESTINAL: 116

    GENITOURINARY: 117

    COMMON IN GERIATRICS: 117

    HEMATOLOGY AND ONCOLOGY: 118

    HEPATIC AND BILIARY: 118

    MUSCULOSKELETAL: 119

    NEUROLOGIC: 119

    PSYCHIATRIC: 120

    PULMONARY: 121

Chapter 20 - Pharmacology - Medications to Review   **123**

Chapter 21 - Physical Assessment - Importance for Nurses **132**

Chapter 22 - Driving Safety For Home Health Nurses   **139**

SECTION 3 – During the Visit   **142**

Being Present with the Patient   **142**

Chapter 23 - Home Safety For Patients and Nurses   **143**

Chapter 24 - The Bag Technique for Home Health Nurses **148**

Chapter 25 - Head to Toe Assessment for Nurses   **157**

Chapter 26 - Medication Reconciliation For Nurses   **167**

Chapter 27 - Some Common Medication Classifications   **173**

Chapter 28 - What Is Durable Medical Equipment (DME)? **187**

Chapter 29 - Nursing Diagnosis   **193**

Chapter 30 - Nursing Interventions   200

Chapter 31 - Psychomotor Skills for Nurses   209

SECTION 4 –   **219**

After the Visit   **219**

Documentation and Communication   **219**

Chapter 32 - Writing a SOAP Note for Registered Nurses   220

**Chapter 33 - Five Star Rating Considerations For Home
Health Agencies**   **225**

Chapter 34 - Quality Assurance in Home Health   **233**

Chapter 35 - Mastering Your Agency's EMR   **239**

**Chapter 36 - The SBAR Communication Technique for
Reporting**   **245**

Chapter 37 - The Role of Case Management in Home Health **250**

Chapter 38 - What is SN in Home Health Skilled Nursing? **257**

Chapter 39 - What Is a Home Health Aide?   **261**

**Chapter 40 - The Role of the Physical Therapist in Home
Health**   **265**

Chapter 41 - What Is Home Health Occupational Therapy? **267**

Chapter 42 - What is a Speech Therapist in Home Health? **272**

Chapter 43 - Medical Social Worker in Home Health   **275**

**Chapter 44 - Director of Nursing (DON/DPCS) in Home
Health**   **278**

Chapter 45 - Primary Care Provider Roles (PCP)   **280**

Chapter 46 - What Is a Primary Caregiver (PCG)   **286**

Chapter 47 - The Role of the Pharmacy   **290**

SECTION 5 – Conclusion   **293**

**Motivating Yourself, Motivating Your Patients, and Motivating
Other Team Members**   **293**

Chapter 48 - What is Motivation?   **294**

Chapter 49 - Motivating Yourself As a Nurse   **297**

Chapter 50 - Strategies For Motivating Your Patients   **303**

Chapter 51 - How to Motivate Your Coworkers   **308**

Chapter 52 - Philosophy of Nursing Ideals and Beliefs   **314**

Chapter 53 - The Importance of Self Care for Nurses   **319**

Chapter 54 - Being a Lifelong Learner As a Nurse   **323**

Appendix A - Download the SOC Checklist Here   **328**

OASISNinja.com   328

Recommended Further Reading   329

    Check out more books by the author at OASISNinja.com   329

Leave a Review!   329

Appendix B - Selected References   **330**

    More books at OASISNinja.com   336

Preface

Welcome to OASIS Ninja: A Home Health Nurse's Guide to Visits, Documentation, and Positive Patient Outcomes.

This book is secretly a motivational book. No amount of technical knowledge will matter if you have no motivation to take action on a consistent basis for years to come in the workplace. Therefore, the last section on motivation may be the most important section you read in this book, besides the technical aspects of nursing it suggests for you to review in the first sections.

The ultimate goal of this book is to orient a new grad nurse into quickly working effectively as a visiting nurse in home health. It assumes that the reader has basic academic knowledge they acquired in a BSN or LVN program, although with no prior experience working formally as a post-undergrad nurse. This is because if you can teach a new grad nurse, then you can teach any nurse regardless of experience level or which specialty they came from.

I originally did research and took notes for myself to help improve my own performance at work as I gained experience working. While I am not perfect, what notes I took down may help other nurses out there, especially ones starting out or changing into this specialty.

One of my philosophies is that competence will lead to confidence and less risk of burnout at work and more job security in the long term. And you will sleep better knowing you made a positive difference in your community. May this book serve you well in your endeavors and good luck in your lifelong learning!

About the Author

Mark Aquino is a registered nurse in California with a Bachelors of Science in Nursing and Masters of Health Administration from West Coast University. He has at least 3 years of experience in the front lines as a visiting nurse in home health, and counting, as he still continues to visit patients at the time of this writing. He is author of OASIS NINJA, a home health nurse's guide to visits, oasis documentation, and positive outcomes for patients. This guide provides nurses with the information they need to provide quality care to their patients in the comfort of their own homes. Learn more at OasisNinja.com.

Recommended Further Reading

Check out more books by the author at OASISNinja.com

Leave a Review!

I would really appreciate it if you would leave a review on Amazon after your purchase and let me know what you think, whether good or bad. It will go a long way in improving the quality of this book and books in the future. Thank you!

SECTION 1 - Fundamentals

The Basics

Chapter 1 - Introduction - What is OASIS

Outcome and Assessment Information Set (OASIS)

If you're a home health care provider, completing the OASIS tool is a must. OASIS Ninja helps clinicians complete the OASIS and provide cost-effective, patient-centered care. This will ensure you are up to speed on the OASIS process.

OASIS stands for Outcome and Assessment Information Set. This patient-specific, standardized assessment tool is used to measure quality and determine reimbursement. Home health providers are required to complete the tool as part of a patient's plan of care. This data set is extensive, and new users can have a difficult time navigating it. When the new Medicare OASIS E1 begins to roll out in 2023, most home health organizations will require field staff to complete OASIS training courses.

In addition to OASIS Ninja training, there are several other online resources that can help home health care practitioners understand the newest OASIS standards. The Centers for Medicare and Medicaid Services have published a new webinar for home health agencies and home health providers. These webinars and Q&A releases will help you meet the compliance requirements for Medicare. When a home health provider uses OASIS, they'll be able to use the latest information on OASIS, including job aids for dressing.

OASIS online charting

The OASIS online charting for home health software helps clinicians conduct OASIS assessments, create a Plan of Care, and complete OBQI and HHRG scoring forms. The software also allows for notes from caregivers and information about the patient's vitals. OASIS also includes features for storing medication interactions, signature capture, and ICD-10 database, as well as a HL-7 interface.

OASIS also helps assess the level of improvement a patient has in his or her ambulation abilities. Patients are measured on a precise zero-to-five scale, and an increased score indicates improvement. This data can help caregivers develop a more effective home health plan. The OASIS online charting for home health software is available for free on the OASIS website. Further, home health agencies can apply the OASIS software to a variety of patient settings.

OASIS online charting for home health is mandatory for non-maternity and pediatric beneficiaries. The tool can be difficult to use at first and requires a thorough training of home health professionals. In addition to ensuring quality care, OASIS online charting for home health can help agencies determine reimbursement. It also helps healthcare organizations measure the quality of home health care and develop a plan of care. But it isn't perfect, and there are still many questions to be answered.

While OASIS has several advantages, it still requires a doctor to sign an order. This order must be related to the patient's primary diagnosis. Physician assistants, Certified Nurse Specialists, and Nurse Practitioners can also sign plan of care. OASIS data sets may vary by state. Therefore, it is important to ensure that data is accurate and comprehensive. Accurate data in OASIS helps the agency receive reimbursements.

OASIS certification

If you're looking to gain the certification of a home health care professional, you can do so by obtaining OASIS-E certification. This updated version of OASIS is effective on Jan. 1, 2023. If you haven't already done so, you need to get a jumpstart on your training. **Axxess offers a comprehensive OASIS-E training series with a four-part Importance of OASIS-D Accuracy and Get Ready for OASIS-E.** This training series includes regulatory overviews, detailed information on comprehensive assessment revisions, and details on the new items.

Having an OASIS certification can boost your credibility in the industry. This certification is not mandatory; however, it can give you an edge when applying for jobs. You can also use educational resources such as reading materials, webinars, and videos to improve your knowledge of the OASIS system. Make sure you are using credible sources when purchasing online educational resources. In addition to reading materials, you can also watch videos or webinars that explain the process of OASIS certification.

Once you obtain OASIS certification, you can apply to home health care agencies in your area to find a job. Some of the companies offer competitive pay and no shift minimums. The more experience you have, the better. If you have a background in the medical field, you should get an OASIS certification for home health care. This will give you an edge in the home care industry. This certification will also help you get the job that you've always wanted to do.

OASIS certification for home health is valuable, but it must be based on a good study. It should focus on real-world practice. This means that factors such as productivity, case management, and agency incentives may affect assessor performance. In addition to OASIS reliability and validity, a study should include data on home health agency staff's training.

Chapter 2 - What is Home Health Care?

What is Home Health Care?

Home health care is medical care that is delivered to a patient's home. It can be used to treat a variety of conditions and is covered by Medicare. It is also referred to as social or domiciliary care. It is a form of skilled care that helps individuals recover from injury, illness, or surgery.

Home health care is medical care delivered directly to a patient's home

Medicare typically covers a variety of health care services, including skilled nursing and rehabilitation. Other benefits include medical social services, durable medical equipment, and medical supplies. Home health care is generally covered at no cost to Medicare beneficiaries, but you may have to pay for certain services yourself. In some cases, you can get extra coverage from other sources, such as Medicare Supplement Insurance. You can also find out if home health care is covered by your insurance plan and what your options are.

Home health care services are designed to maintain a patient's quality of life and slow the rate of decline in health. Many patients and family members benefit from receiving medical care in the comfort of their own home. This reduces hospital bills and increases the likelihood of a patient staying in his or her home for as long as possible.

When applying for home health care, your physician will need to approve your request. Home health agencies are required to have a written care plan for their patients. The plan is developed by the home health agency with input from the patient and family. Once approved, the care plan is updated on a regular basis and provided by the home health agency. In addition, home health agencies must disclose financial ties to insurance companies.

The benefits are compelling. In fact, home health care has increased the use of Medicare reimbursement, and the number of patients receiving such services is on the rise. The costs of hospitalization have increased, and many patients need to avoid expensive care when they are in their own home. A study by Cleveland Clinic researchers found that patients receiving home health services were less likely to be readmitted to the hospital and died during a hospital stay, saving $6,500 annually.

While home health care provides a more personalized approach to care, research on the effectiveness of such services is limited. Although costs of home health care are lower than those of inpatient hospitalization, the cost of personal care can be higher. The quality of care and communication between physicians and staff members are both important.

It is a type of skilled care

Home health care is a popular choice for seniors in need of care. These health professionals provide a range of different services, such as medication management and assistance with activities of daily living. However, unlike skilled nursing care, which is typically provided in a hospital, home health is provided in the home. Home health services are hired on an as-needed basis. Here are some benefits of this option. The most important factor is the level of care provided.

The goal of home health is to provide skilled medical care to patients in their own homes. These services may include **skilled nursing, social worker, physical, occupational, speech therapy, and home health aide**. Home health providers will send a licensed professional to the patient's home to assess their needs and develop a comprehensive care plan.

Most home health care services are temporary, but some are covered by Medicaid or long-term insurance. Medicare also covers these services for patients who cannot afford them.

Before a loved one can receive home health care, he or she must meet with a physician. The physician must complete a home health certification form, which identifies the patient's homebound status and needs for intermittent skilled care. The physician should also approve the plan of care. The plan must be reviewed by both the physician and the patient. The physician is the best person to determine whether home health care services are right for your loved one.

The most obvious benefit of home health is that the caregiver can spend more time with their loved one and less time at the hospital. Home health services provide a wide range of services, including postoperative wound care, intravenous therapy, nutrition therapy, injections, and patient and caregiver education. Many home health services are based on a plan of care that outlines specific procedures and treatment options. You should also consider when Medicare coverage ends. Some home health care agencies will be closed after Medicare coverage expires, and you will need to find a new agency.

It is covered by Medicare

Medicare covers some types of home health care. Some of these services include skilled nursing care, rehabilitative care, and physical therapy. Some services include medical social services, occupational therapy, speech-language pathology, and even medical supplies. Telehealth is also covered by Medicare in certain cases, but it can be tricky to qualify. Medicare also helps people afford the cost of health care, and home health care services are often a great option for recovering patients.

Original Medicare pays for the cost of home health care for anyone who qualifies. Medicare Advantage plans can vary in cost, rules, and benefits. Original Medicare covers home health care costs 100%. However, some of the Medicare Advantage plans require you to pay a copayment for home health care services. Therefore, it is important to check the fine print carefully before signing up for a Medicare Advantage plan. Some plans may have a deductible or co-insurance that limits the amount of home health care you can receive.

Whether or not home health care is covered by Medicare depends on whether the patient meets certain criteria. The Medicare home health benefit covers **intermittent** skilled nursing care, therapy, and social services provided by a home health aide. To receive Medicare coverage for home health care, the service provider must be certified through the Medicare program. The patient must sign up for services within a month of the service start date. Medicare only covers home health services from an approved agency.

Home health aides are specially trained individuals that assist individuals with their needs at home. These aides can assist with bathing, dressing, and other activities of daily living. Medicare will cover the cost of personal care aides when they are part of a package of home health services. These services can also include physical therapy and occupational therapy. A home health agency must meet strict regulations to be certified and approved by Medicare.

It can help people recover from illness, operation, or injury

Home health is a service that offers medical assistance to people in the comfort of their own home after an illness, operation, or injury. Trained professionals provide medical assistance and physical therapy to patients, helping them recover faster and with fewer complications. Home health professionals may also offer social and educational support. Moreover, home health services can reduce the risk of errors and other complications, such as medication errors or falling.

In home health, nurses provide assistance to people recovering from an illness or injury. They assist the patients with wound care, administer medication, and assist with other daily activities. Aside from nurses, home health aides also provide personal care and help with light housekeeping. Physical and occupational therapists, social workers, and speech language pathologists also provide services to patients, which may be covered by insurance.

Chapter 3 - What Makes a Great Home Health Nurse?

If you are considering a career in home health care, here are some things to keep in mind: flexibility, organization, and relationship-building skills. Here are some of the skills you'll need to be a successful home health nurse. These qualities will not only make you a great nurse, but they will help you get the job done. These are just a few of the many qualities that make a home health nurse great.

Skills needed

There are several skills you should have as a home health nurse. This job requires you to be able to communicate effectively. You will be expected to convey information to patients in a clear, concise manner and to develop trust with patients and their families. Likewise, you will need to be able to switch between layman and medical jargon when interacting with patients. These skills can help you enhance your relationship with patients and foster better care.

Physical stamina, flexibility, and a high level of mental strength are required to work as a home health nurse. Depending on the type of patients you see, you may be required to perform regular physical tasks. You should be compassionate and sensitive to the emotions of patients and families. You should be organized, detail-oriented, and able to handle multiple tasks at once. The job also requires a high degree of physical stamina, especially when dealing with patients who are ill or in pain.

As a home health nurse, you will be interacting one-on-one with patients, enabling you to develop a stronger connection with them. Home health nurses also have the advantage of working in a much more personal setting compared to a hospital or medical office. For this reason, many home health nurses choose to work part-time or even full-time, allowing them to earn a higher income while working at home.

As a home health nurse, you will be responsible for providing skilled nursing care in patients' homes. In addition to providing care, your role also involves assisting the family with self-care. Home health nurses also monitor the patient's physiological condition and safety. Throughout the job, you will be responsible for developing and implementing care plans, developing patient-centered care, and exchanging information with appropriate medical staff.

Flexibility

What makes a good home health nurse? Flexibility. Home health nurses work with patients in their own homes and form strong relationships. They have plenty of autonomy and are generally motivated self-starters. The role requires good communication and organizational skills. A great home health nurse should be confident in her ability to perform her duties and assert her patients' needs. Flexibility in your work environment is essential for patient safety and satisfaction.

Advanced communication skills. In home care nursing, nurses are often responsible for working with patients, often patients who do not speak English very well or are unable to understand basic instructions. They must be able to listen to patients and be flexible and responsive in unexpected situations. In addition to having excellent communication skills, home health nurses must be physically fit to withstand the demands of the job. As a result, they need to have an advanced understanding of human behavior.

Flexible workplace. Flexible work schedules enable nurses to make the most of their time. Flexible working conditions can be created through creative thinking. Flexible working hours can be set up so that a nurse can fit work and home life. This type of schedule will be more complicated, but can be designed with input from other healthcare professionals. Flexibility also enhances the ability to develop a relationship with patients and the community. As a result, home health nurses are often better suited to help the elderly and other patients who are not able to leave their homes.

Depending on the agency, a home health nurse can work traditional hours or flexible hours. Some home health nurses work overnight, while others work four days a week. The latter option can also be flexible. Depending on the agency, a home health nurse can work weekends and holidays. This flexibility allows nurses to schedule their own personal appointments, as well as other activities throughout the day. A home health nurse must be able to make clinical decisions while working with patients. In this role, nurses must apply their assessment and teaching skills on a daily basis.

Organization

Nurses are often faced with a variety of responsibilities, including delivering high-quality care. In home health care, nurses often must make decisions based on multiple factors including patient condition, engagement, and caregiver availability. **A recent study reviewed the decision-making processes and strategies of 26 home health nurses at three agencies. Findings revealed that nurses developed personalized visit plans based on the needs of their patients and then revised them as necessary based on patient condition, engagement, and availability.** The study also identified strategies to improve visit planning to positively influence patient outcomes.

Magnet-recognized organizations involve nurses in decision-making processes, ensuring that they work collaboratively with other disciplines. Nurses in Magnet-recognized organizations demonstrate high-quality patient care and collaboration, as well as collaboration with other disciplines to provide integrated, coordinated care. They measure patient outcomes and develop strong partnerships with community organizations. They engage in evidence-based practice and use national benchmarks to measure outcomes.

An effective home health nurse exhibits leadership skills. She can inspire the team by sharing a vision and fostering a collaborative environment. She can also be a great mentor and educator, and she can encourage and inspire others to develop their own skills. She may even choose to earn a doctorate and further her education through certification. And because of her compassion and care, she is often the only one who can provide the best care in the home for a patient.

In addition to patient-centered care, an effective home health nurse fosters a collaborative relationship with patients. The nurse also builds trust with patients by documenting the patterns of the visits. During the visit, she assesses patient eligibility and ensures that all patients receive appropriate care. If the patient is not engaged in their care, the nurse informs the patient and the physical therapist, and if necessary, reactivates the skilled nursing services.

Relationship-building skills

Good communication skills are an essential tool for a home health nurse. Effective communication skills help the nurse convey information to patients and foster trust. Good interpersonal skills can also help the nurse provide high-quality care. Active listening skills can be strengthened through reading books or taking online training resources. Active listening skills are essential in home health nursing, as they allow flexibility and adaptation to the work environment. Moreover, home health nurses need to be flexible and adaptable to patient needs and preferences.

As a home health nurse, you will be working closely with patients. Your patient's health is a primary concern and your job is to make them feel comfortable. This means that you must learn to develop positive relationships with your patients. By asking questions and getting to know their personal lives, you can make them feel more comfortable and find the best treatments for their conditions. Relationship-building skills are essential for the successful career in home health nursing.

You should have excellent interpersonal skills, as these skills are essential for a successful career in home care. The ability to listen to patients and understand them, and expressing care and concern is essential. By developing relationships with your patients, you can improve their health and well-being. If you're passionate about your work, you'll be able to develop relationships that will last a lifetime. Relationship-building skills make a great home health nurse, so develop them as much as you can and see if they will be your top priority.

Good communication skills are essential for establishing rapport with patients. By developing trust, you'll be able to better understand their feelings and understand the needs and preferences of their patients. With the ability to communicate effectively with patients, rapport is a vital component for improving care. Rapport-building skills are not universal, so you'll need to learn how to build rapport with each patient. You need to consider each patient's communication preferences, and adapt your communication style to make it work best.

Independence

As a home health nurse, you are part of a larger care team, but you must still have independence to carry out your job well. Home health nurses work in a setting that is not always conducive to a traditional setting, which requires an extra level of adaptability and critical thinking. You'll meet patients in their homes, which can be unnerving for a patient if they're not used to interacting with outside professionals. Luckily, the independence of working in a home-based setting makes it an ideal career for nurses.

Working in a home-based setting allows nurses to gain experience by working directly with patients. The freedom of home-based care means nurses can take their time and learn more about patients' needs. They can also earn a bachelor's degree while working as a home health nurse. A home-based nursing job is rewarding for both the nurse and the patient. It's important to consider the pros and cons of the job before making a final decision.

An independence-oriented home health nurse can choose to work a more traditional job or a more flexible schedule. Some nurses work overnight or on weekends. Depending on the agency, you can choose your hours. Home health nurses can work four days a week or even on weekends. The work schedule is completely up to you, and you'll have more freedom to determine how much time you want to spend with your patient. Home health nurses must be compassionate, knowledgeable, and dependable.

Chapter 4 - Home Health and CMS (Centers for Medicare & Medicaid Services)

The Centers for Medicare & Medicaid Services are federal agencies within the U.S. Department of Health and Human Services that administer the Medicare program. They work with other federal agencies to ensure that people have access to health care.

Quality control

Among the many responsibilities of the Centers for Medicare & Medicaid Services (CMS) is the development of quality measures. CMS uses these measures in its public reporting and pay-for-reporting programs. The agency is also responsible for overseeing and investigating complaints of fraud and abuse. It also aims to provide high-quality care to Medicare beneficiaries and their families.

Advocates and consumers are increasingly interested in quality in healthcare. Quality is integral to understanding who receives care, ensuring appropriateness and promptness of care, and exploring systemic reasons for quality issues. Quality standards can be translated into practiced norms by creating a culture that encourages quality care and patient safety.

While pay-for-performance initially promoted as a quality improvement method, it has now been embraced as a cost containment tool. Many health plans believe that rising health care costs are the result of overutilization and are therefore trying to limit unnecessary medical procedures

Quality measures

As the home health industry continues to move toward value-based care, payers must be aware of the quality measures available to measure performance. Historically, CMS has been an early adopter of these measures, but private payers are not bound to replicate them. Quality measures in home health are based on the six domains of health care quality identified by the Institute of Medicine. They focus on patient-centeredness, patient engagement, and effectiveness of outreach strategies.

The quality measures for home health should include a number of specific and reliable measures, which are designed to measure the quality of care provided. Process measures may include timely initiation of care, depression assessment, fall risk assessments, medication education, and influenza immunization status. The quality measures must also adjust for member characteristics, since the reasons for readmission can vary widely. In addition, CMS requires providers to report claims data, which are used to determine quality.

In March 2019, CMS released details on its planned changes to quality measure rating thresholds. The new thresholds would increase every six months by 50% of the rate at which QM ratings improve. That would increase the threshold by 1%, for example. The goal is to encourage continuous quality improvement and limit future threshold adjustments. These threshold changes were originally scheduled for April 2020, but were halted due to the COVID-19 Public Health Emergency.

You can also find more information about the measures by reading the Technical Documentation for OASIS-based Measures. Alternatively, if you aren't familiar with PAE measures, you can consult the Outcome-Based Quality Monitoring Manual. It lists the requirements for home health agencies and allows you to compare them nationally.

CMS has been delaying the release of its updated OASIS. Home health agencies will be required to begin collecting data on the updated item sets on January 1, 2023. While the new quality measures are still in development, there are already a few benchmarks in place. Using these metrics will help payers better understand the quality of their care and identify areas for improvement. You can find the Final Rule in the Federal Registrar.

Chapter 5 - Changes to OASIS E-1 Documentation

There are changes to OASIS and how they may affect agencies and clinicians. Changes start after January 1, 2023. This section discusses validity, generalizability, and reliability. We discuss each of these aspects in more detail.

Changes to OASIS

The OASIS-E instrument is the next step in the implementation process. It will capture data for several measures, including the Transfer of Health Information to Provider-PAC and Standardized Patient Assessment Data Elements. The changes were delayed to ensure maximum flexibility for providers. They are effective January 1, 2021, and will be finalized with the Office of Management and Budget. If you are planning to implement this new instrument, you should familiarize yourself with the new structure before implementing it.

As of January 1, 2019, OASIS-E is undergoing change, including changes in the guidance and a few new items. You should start preparing early to ensure that you are prepared for this important change. A thorough OASIS training will focus on the changes. The Ultimate OASIS-E virtual training will take you through all items. You can also get the guidance and support you need to complete the new form as early as 2023.

A composite change methodology places all OASIS items on the same playing field. For example, the ambulation question contains six levels of change. For example, starting from six means your patient is not ambulatory, and improving to zero will result in improvement of six levels. There are no such levels for other OASIS items. It is important to note that the OASIS was designed with the ambulation question in mind.

In addition to the modifications to the OASIS, the newest version includes an evidence-based screening tool, the PHQ-2. While this tool is embedded in the OASIS, it is not mandatory. This means home health clinicians can use other tools to assess patients for depression. Although these changes are expected to improve the reliability of the questionnaire, further studies are necessary to determine the impact of the OASIS on clinical outcomes.

While implementing the new OASIS-E is relatively simple, there is a steep learning curve to get through. It is not the typical "train the trainer" scenario; instead, the process will involve a whole agency's staff. Once it is official, everyone should take the time to get up to speed on the new items. Home health agencies should make a plan for learning new items and implementing the changes.

Reliability

Despite recent developments in medical care, there is still considerable uncertainty regarding OASIS reliability and validity. Studies have shown low reliability and validity for some OASIS items, raising questions about their usefulness in outcome measurement. In particular, these findings highlight the unidimensional nature of the OASIS's functional, behavioral, and affect domains. The use of response categories for functional items may be problematic, and combining scores for different disability domains may not be valid.

The lack of standardized testing and a limited number of studies demonstrates that OASIS cannot be used for longitudinal research. Additionally, the limited number of studies available for the various OASIS versions does not allow researchers to establish the validity and reliability of individual items and composite scores. Researchers must therefore exercise caution when using OASIS data to investigate differences in outcome, contributing factors, and disparities.

For this reason, future studies should address the issue of OASIS reliability and validity.

OASIS was not designed to be a comprehensive assessment tool. It is used in three phases: at the beginning of care, at 60-day follow-ups, and at discharge. Because of the limited number of items, home health agencies will likely need to supplement OASIS items with other assessment tools. Moreover, OASIS does not measure vital signs, which are an important aspect of patient care.

A systematic literature review of OASIS data has revealed that there is a lack of consensus on the validity and reliability of OASIS. While there is no uniform standard, most studies report a wide range of results. However, some studies failed to address other important issues, including the reliability of OASIS scores. One study even found that OASIS scores were higher for home health care agencies than for other health care settings.

Validity

The validity of OASIS items varies from study to study. In general, they have high validity rates, with Cronbach's alpha of .87 or higher. However, there are several factors that can influence OASIS item by item validity. Moreover, patients who use OASIS items may have a variety of different needs. As such, additional studies are necessary to confirm these results. In any case, validating OASIS with an item-by-item system is highly recommended.

The OASIS is valid for the ADLs and cognitive status appraisal, but may not be sensitive enough for the IADLs and depressive symptoms. The IADLs represent a persistent challenge, and the items that measure those challenges are important for the assessment of depression. However, it is important to follow the recommendations for this assessment in case of severe depression. This study was supported by the National Institute of Nursing Research, grant number NR005081.

The study was part of a larger study that examined factors associated with health outcomes in Medicare home health care patients. Twenty-eight Ohio Medicare-certified home health agencies participated in the study. During these visits, these RNs attempted to interview consented patients. A systematic review of the existing studies found 12 articles on OASIS item by item validity. This research was limited by the nonrepresentative nature of the sample.

The OASIS data interchange protocol is the standard for the exchange of health care data. It has become a standard across the U.S. healthcare system. The OASIS protocol was designed by the National Institute of Health (NIH) to make sure that health care providers are compliant with federal and state guidelines. OASIS-D1 is the latest version. It includes information about the requirements and standards of the system.

Generalizability

There are some important issues regarding the generalizability of OASIS item-by-item scores. The items tested, statistical procedures, and methods used in the OASIS have not been consistently applied throughout the years. There are also several differences in coding instructions. The results are only tentative and additional studies are needed to confirm them. The OASIS is a valuable tool in assessing patient outcomes, research, and quality improvement.

The OASIS stimulus set contains 900 open-access images normed on two affective dimensions. This database contains two distinct affective dimensions: valence and arousal. Both are measures of the positivity or negativity of an image. The valence scale contains three meaningful anchor points that can be used to generalize the results. Compared to other visual stimuli, the OASIS image sets are the most generalizable.

While studies have generally produced similar results, their interpretations of the findings may differ. Expert reviews are needed to develop standards for acceptable levels of reliability and validity. Such standards can be used to refine OASIS over time. Unfortunately, the studies do not examine the accuracy of OASIS completion and the training of staff in home health agencies. Several differences were found between therapy and nursing. These findings should be a cause for concern for future studies.

It is important to note that the OASIS does not have a large number of studies. A multistage probability sampling design would be more useful for validating individual OASIS items, although this approach would not necessarily improve point estimates. Although the study participants' experience was highly diverse, OASIS items demonstrated strong correlations with anxiety measures, including behavioral and clinician-rated anxiety severity. However, further studies need to evaluate the convergence of OASIS scores with these outcome measures.

Although OASIS is used extensively in clinical practice, very few studies have examined the psychometric properties of the scale. It should be tested within the context of home healthcare, where variables such as productivity, case management, and agency incentives may have an impact on the score. Likewise, studies should consider the generalizability of OASIS item by item scores compared to the CMS 485.

Chapter 6 - What is OASIS E-1?

OASIS E-1 is one of the new standards set by OASIS. This certification will be given to individuals with a range of physical disabilities. It has multiple items with multiple letters, including questions on ethnicity, language, transportation, hearing, vision, and pain in activity. The new version will also remove the M item regarding pain during activity and replace it with J items. This will require a lot of education and training.

OASIS-D1

OASIS-D1 and OASIS-E are two OASIS forms. The first one is based on the older version of the assessment tool, and the newer version is designed to measure the same things, but with updated guidance and 25 percent of the assessments' items. The revision will also change the item numbers and sectional structure, and it will align with other data assessment systems used in post-acute care settings. This version will also retire several items, including M1200 Vision, M1242 Interfering Pain, and M2016 Drug Education.

As the new version of the assessment takes effect on Jan. 1, 2021, the OASIS data set will undergo dramatic changes. Though the implementation of OASIS-E has been delayed due to the COVID-19 Public Health emergency, it is expected to be finalized by 2023. However, organizations must be prepared for the transition and its implications. In addition to changes in data collection and reporting standards, OASIS-D1 and OASIS-E will require a new assessment structure.

The new OASIS assessment will have the same goals, but will be based on social determinants of health. These factors will affect care and payment. By identifying social determinants of health, organizations will be better equipped to address patient needs.

In addition, these factors can bridge the gap between the quality of care and the quality of outcomes. Moreover, the new assessment is consistent with other CMS initiatives and focuses on holistic care.

OASIS-D1 is the best option for supervisors and QA staff that are preparing for the COS-C exam. OASIS-D1 and OASIS E-1 can be combined with a certification program to provide a complete course for healthcare professionals. This course consists of 16 lessons, each with a handout, video demonstration, and post-quizzes. The course is available in bulk for multiple users. **McBee** offers bulk licensing options for multiple users.

OASIS-D1 and OASIS-E have similar structure and function, but the OASIS-D1 has more detailed information on the new standardized OASIS. The new version also supports the IMPACT Act of 2014 and adds two SPADEs elements. Although the OASIS-D1 data set is similar, it differs from the OASIS-E in appearance and flow.

OASIS-D1 transitional component

Implementing the OASIS-D1 transitional component is a vital part of the agency quality process. This component will help your agency measure clinician insight, engagement, and satisfaction. However, it is important to note that it may seem counterintuitive to train clinicians on OASIS-D1 items too early. After all, they won't be using them for months. That said, the benefits of this approach are significant.

As part of the OASIS-D1 transitional component, many current assessment items will be retained, but with a different character designation. They will be moved into a lettered section, based on the part of the body they represent. For example, Section M will represent the integumentary system. Items that pertain to wounds, such as M1720, "When Anxious," will remain in Section C.

For the OASIS-D1 transitional component, CMS requires providers to document a change in a primary diagnosis and other diagnoses. A medical necessity documentation is needed. The documentation that accompanies an OASIS-D1 transitional component is essential to the reimbursement process. OASIS documentation must be accurate to support medical necessity and case mix weight. The OASIS-D1 transitional component is the perfect tool to get started on the right foot.

OASIS-D1's main changes were made to make the standards more consistent with the IMPACT Act. The OASIS-D1 transitional component, also known as OASIS-D1, aims to create a standard for health information and the corresponding medical data. It has similarities with the MDS data set. It is important for organizations to understand the impact of this transition on OASIS data.

Future research on the OASIS-D1 transitional component should consider whether the measures are generalizable and how to make them more reliable. Current studies used nonrepresentative samples, and a multistage probability sampling design would increase confidence in validity and reliability inferences. More representative samples would also decrease sampling error, but they would not necessarily lead to better point estimates. But it is important to note that the OASIS-D1 transitional component will become effective after January 1, 2020.

The OASIS-D1 transitional component is important because it serves both resumption and recert functions. It should be completed accurately and fully to contribute to an integrated discharge plan. By doing so, the OASIS assessment will contribute to coordinating an integrated discharge plan. And as long as it meets these two critical criteria, OASIS-D1 will continue to be an important part of the CMS's integrated care system.

OASIS-E implementation date

CMS recently bumped up the OASIS-E implementation date from Jan. 1, 2021, to January 1, 2023, due to the COVID-19 public health emergency. The new rule will require HHAs to use OASIS-E beginning with discharges on or after January 1, 2023. CMS also published an interim final rule in the Federal Register on May 8, 2020, which will cut short the PHE reprieve and set the OASIS-E implementation date for January 1, 2023.

CMS has continued to fine-tune OASIS-E, including the separation of race and ethnicity questions. It has also removed Item M2016 and added the "Patient declines to respond" option. While the Office of Management and Budget has not yet approved the new version of OASIS-E, SimiTree consultants caution against making additional changes. In the meantime, home health providers should take advantage of OASIS-E accuracy training sessions to become compliant.

The Centers for Medicare & Medicaid Services released the latest OASIS Q&As, providing guidance to OASIS questions submitted through their help desk. OASIS Q&As cover topics ranging from updates to coding M and GG items to guidelines for confusing scenarios. Here are the highlights of the 14 Q&As. If you are planning to use OASIS-E, make sure you know the deadline and how to prepare. The OASIS-E implementation date has a huge impact on the home health industry.

In the end, the OASIS-E implementation date is just around the corner, and your actions today will be crucial to the future success of your organization. With so many changes brewing in health care, ensuring that your team is ready is key. In fact, almost 40% of agencies don't have an OASIS-E education plan.

You can find out more about the deadline and the OASIS-E education requirements by browsing our blog.

OASIS-E is aligned with CMS' other initiatives. It focuses on the holistic nature of health care delivery. By collecting data elements related to social determinants of health, an organization can address the needs of each patient. As a result, they can help reduce healthcare disparities. The OASIS-E implementation date is set for January 1, 2023. The proposed changes are significant revisions to the OASIS-D1 items, and a new response option.

OASIS-E education

Implementation of the OASIS-E is expected to begin by the end of this year. As of this writing, only 15% of agencies plan to implement the OASIS-E. This means that the majority of agencies will still train their staffs using the previous manual. Regardless of the implementation date, agencies should focus on transitional aspects of OASIS-E education and training. In addition to this, the transitional items of the OASIS-E are likely to increase clinician insight, engagement, and satisfaction.

Although there are many new OASIS-E items in the final version, many current assessment items will retain their character designation of "M." These items will still be included in the corresponding lettered section of the OASIS-E. Section M represents the integumentary system. As a result, only "M" items related to wounds will be included in this section. Thus, the item M1720, "When Anxious," will remain in Section C.

The OASIS-E manual has detailed information on items, including tips on answering specific questions. Chapter 3 is devoted to the transitional process for data elements and will help clinicians assess their patients. For more detailed descriptions of the changes made from OASIS D1 to OASIS-E, refer to Appendix D. This section contains a chart with a summary of the changes and new items since the D1 version.

OASIS-E is an important step toward achieving the broader CMS objectives for quality care. It requires organizations to collect information about the social determinants of health, and the results of this process will help them identify and address the needs of individual patients. By doing so, organizations will be better equipped to treat patients and reduce the disparities in care. So, as home health agencies prepare for the OASIS-E, they should focus on this important task.

The OASIS-E will be implemented nationwide on January 1, 2023. Home health agencies will transition to the new system by 2023, though the onset of the implementation was delayed due to a COVID-19 public health emergency. OASIS-E data will directly impact patient outcomes and payment, so it's vital for providers to understand how to use this new system. This update represents one of the most important changes to the industry in years.

Chapter 7 - New OASIS Items and Retired Items

OASIS E-1 is a nationally implemented instrument that has 27 new items. This update will add several new items and make the entire tool more reliable. In addition, the new instruments will add more letters to the OASIS score, improving its validity and reducing the need for re-tests.

OASIS-E is a nationally implemented instrument

The Centers for Medicare and Medicaid Services (CMS) delayed the implementation of the OASIS-E by two years, from January 1, 2021 to January 1, 2022. This is good news for home health agencies, as they have been undergoing significant disruption from COVID-19, a Public Health Emergency. The delay also allows home health agencies to continue with existing COVID-19 projects, such as developing new home care services.

In addition to improving communication between clinicians and patients, OASIS is important for assessing infection rates. This new instrument will help healthcare providers determine a course of treatment for a patient's infection. It will also increase infection detection rates and monitor surgical wounds. This instrument is also free to use in hospitals and health systems nationwide. While there are still many questions about how to use OASIS, a key component is ensuring that it is used as intended.

To prepare for OASIS-E implementation, agencies must educate themselves on the new instrument. A technical assistance call was hosted by CMMI on Feb. 10th. You can access the recording of the call here. There are several resources related to the HHVBP, including the OASIS-E manual. CMS also finalized the implementation date for OASIS-E, which is now scheduled for Jan. 1, 2023. During the Public Health Emergency, the implementation date was delayed by a year to provide flexibility. However, the updated draft of OASIS-E can now be downloaded from the OASIS Data Sets webpage. The Office of Management and Budget must approve the instrument's implementation.

Despite its high level of reliability, the OASIS-E has some limitations. It lacks consistency in the method of testing individual items and composites. Further, it lacks the number of studies to prove its validity. Therefore, researchers should be cautious when using OASIS data to investigate disparities and contributing factors. The validity of subscales is another area that needs to be evaluated. If a study fails to use OASIS-E data, researchers should consider conducting an independent review.

It has 27 new items and will retire 9 old items

The OASIS assessment tool has undergone an overhaul. **It now includes an additional 27 items that were not previously covered. It will also retire 9 items.** In addition to the new items, the OASIS Assessment Tool also requires agencies to indicate a current medication list to subsequent providers. The OASIS Assessment Tool is a useful reminder to stay on top of your OASIS training. But what exactly is new?

27 New Items:

A1005 - Ethnicity

A1010 - Race

A1100 - Language

A1250 - Transportation

A2120 - Provision of Current Reconciled Medication List to Subsequent Provider at Transfer

A2121 - Provision of Current Reconciled Medication List to Subsequent Provider @ D/C

A2122 - Route of Current Reconciled Medication List Transmission to Subsequent Provider

A2123 - Provision of Current Reconciled Medication List to Patient at Discharge

A2124 - Route of Current Reconciled Medication List Transmission to Patient

B0200 - Hearing

B1000 - Vision

B1300 - Health Literacy

C0100 - Should Brief Interview for Mental Status be Conducted

C0200 - Repetition of Three Words

C0300 - Temporal Orientation

C0400 - Recall

C0500 - BIMS Summary Score

C1310 - Signs and Symptoms of Delirium

D0150 - Patient Mood Interview

D0160 - Total Severity Score

D0700 - Social Isolation

J0510 - Pain Effect on Sleep

J0520 - Pain Interference with Therapy Activities

J0530 - Pain Interference with Day-to-Day Activities

K0520 - Nutritional Approaches

N0415 - High-Risk Drug Classes: Use and Indication

O0110 - Special Treatments, Procedures and Programs

CMS has released a draft version of the assessment, but OMB hasn't approved it yet. However, it is expected to be approved this year. In the meantime, CMS released a crosswalk of OASIS-D to OASIS-E, which details the new assessment's 27 new items. The final rule details these changes.

The OASIS-D1 and OASIS-E assessment forms will be used for reporting purposes. However, the new OASIS-E assessment form is designed to be more accurate and consistent. Its changes will make it easier for healthcare providers to compare their data and improve patient care. In addition, it will enable agencies to compare their quality metrics in a single, standardized form. The changes will also streamline the reporting process for all agencies.

9 Items To Be Retired:

M0140 - Race / Ethnicity

M1030 - Therapies at Home

M1051/M1056 - Pneumococcal Vaccine

M1200 - Vision

M1242 - Pain Interfering with Activity

M1730 - Depression Screening

M1910 - Fall Risk

M2016 - Patient / Caregiver Drug Education Intervention

It will have multiple letters

The new OASIS-E has 27 new items. For reference, the letters "E" and "M" represent different aspects of a patient's health. For example, "M1720" stands for "When Anxious" and will be in

Section C. The BIMS section will measure patients' cognitive patterns and mood, while the "E" letter will be used for a more holistic view of a patient's health.

OASIS-E is one of the most significant changes to the OASIS data set. To prepare for OASIS-E, organizations must understand its scope and what it entails. There are also several other changes. To understand what changes are made, read the OASIS E manual in the CMS website.

Agencies must decide where to get education and how to educate staff on the changes. Education sessions are ongoing at state and national association conferences and should start in October. During these sessions, staff should be educated on the new OASIS-E standards. It is imperative to begin these sessions as soon as possible.

It will improve validity

OASIS E will include new standardized patient assessment data elements that will assess pain, cognition, continence, and mobility. It will also assess falls. It will also have new sections for cognition and pain, and it will also have a new scale for pain.

The OASIS-E is scheduled to introduce new sections, including the BIMS section. BIMS measures cognitive patterns, behavioral responses, and mood. Once complete, OASIS-E will become mandatory for all HHAs and skilled care programs that accept Medicare. These changes will improve the validity of the assessment and the quality of care that the patients receive. You can use OASIS E in conjunction with a number of new tools and programs to help you improve the accuracy of your clinical trials.

In addition to addressing the accuracy and completeness of OASIS, these studies also need to consider the real-world practice context. The differences in productivity, case management, and agency incentives are known to affect assessor performance. For example, a recent study by Madigan et al. found discrepancies between the two scales, and that these discrepancies affected the outcome of the patient's care. Home care agencies may be motivated to make patients appear more sick or injured than they are, which could affect the validity of the nationally implemented instrument.

It will improve employee engagement

While OASIS-E has been on the horizon for a while, the pandemic kept the implementation date off. Healthcare providers had other things to worry about, but now that the pandemic has passed, OASIS-E is top of mind.

Chapter 8 - The SOC Checklist in SOAP Format

Below is a sample checklist in SOAP format for gathering OASIS data that I personally use which I have customized for my needs. I bring this checklist with me every patient visit and go through this checklist every time so that I do not miss anything.

According to the book *Checklist Manifesto: How to Get Things Right* by Atul Gawande, checklists are great for improving job performance in the workplace. In my personal experience, having a comprehensive checklist puts me at ease and reduces my anxiety knowing that I have a reference and guide to all things I need to cover during the day.

But be warned that as you go through the process of referencing your checklist day to day, you may notice that after a few weeks or after a few months of using the checklist daily, you start getting into a habit and the checklist starts becoming a mental checklist for you.

Be careful when the physical checklist starts becoming a mental checklist, so that you do not become prideful and start making mistakes. Relying on a mental checklist is a recipe for disaster, as the human mind is prone to error. Always rely on a physical copy of a checklist, whether on paper or digitally, to do your job right.

Let this template be a guide for you to create your own checklist as you see fit, or use this checklist as is for your own practice.

Comprehensive SOC Checklist:

<table>
<tr><td></td><td>
Patient Name: Date:

MD/DO:

Reason for Visit: SOC, ROC, Recert, F/U, DC
</td></tr>
<tr><td>S</td><td>
From: Community/Hospital/SNF

DC Date:

LOS:

Reason for referral (CC):

PMHx:

PSHx:

HPI (OLDCART):

Diabetes, PAD, or PVD?

IV Access Y/N

Oral: indep/setup/reminder/unable/NA

Injectable: indep/setup/reminder/unable/NA

Medications (MED LIST):

Drug Issues:

Allergies:

Limitations: Amputation, Dyspnea, Paralysis, Contracture, Blind, Incontinent, Hearing, Endurance, Speech

Lives: Alone, w/Someone, ALF

Assistance Available: Around Clock, Day, Night, Short Term, None ///
</td></tr>
</table>

PCG name & contact:

Community/Social Screening: Needs resources, Sadness, Suicidal, Suspected Abuse/Neglect For:

MSW Needed: Y/N

Home Safety: Stairs, No running water; poor lighting, heat, or cool; narrow or obstructed walkways, insects/rodents, no fire safety, cluttered/soiled, Other:

O2 Safety Y/N: NA, No Smoking Signs, Smoke inside, Smoke Detectors, Fire Extinguisher, Safe Cylinder Storage, Cords Intact, Evacuation Plan, Cleaning Fluids, No petroleum products, Only water-based lip moisturizers

Pain:

Code Status: DNR/Full code

Adv Directives:

Vaccines: Flu, Pneumonia, Shingles, TB

VS: BP: PP: Temp: Resp: O2:

Ht:

Wt:

O   BS: Labs (if any):

HEAD TO TOE ASSESSMENT/REVIEW OF SYSTEMS:

Sensory: Eyes/Vision: Poor vision? Y/N   Ears: HOH? Y/N   Nose: Nasal obstruction? Y/N

Neuro: Oriented: Person Place Time, Disoriented, Forgetful, PERRL, Seizures, Tremors

Psychosocial: Poor Environment, Poor Coping, Agitated, Depressed, Impaired Decision-Making, Anxiety, Inappropriate Behavior, Irritability   **PHQ-2:** Last two weeks, Little interest or pleasure in doing things? Feeling Down, depressed, or hopeless

Lungs: SOB, Supplemental O2, O2 Sat, Cough,   **Auscultation** lung fields: Adventitious lung sounds? Y/N

Cardiac: Chest Pain, Dizziness, Edema, Heart Sounds, Peripheral Pulses,   Cap Refill <3, >3 Pacemaker. AICD

Bowels: Incontinen Freq   **Ostomy:**   **Dialysis** Hemo, Graft/Fistula Site: CVC Site: Peritoneal Signs of infection Y/N

Nutrition: Dysphagia, Poor Appetite, Wt Loss/Gain: **Diet:** Adequate Y/N **Problems:** Throat, Dental, Dentures, Chewing, Other:

Urinary: Incontinence, Distention, Burning, Frequency, Dysuria, Retention, Urgency, Urostomy **Catheter** Last Changed: Cloudy, Odorous, Sediment, Hematuria   **Genitalia:**

Skin: Wounds:

Diabetes: Insulin, pt/cg draw dose/administer, oral hypoglycemic, pt/cg indep with glucometer, inspect feet   **Blood Sugar:**

Other Endocrine: Polyuria, Polydipsia, Polyphagia, Neuropathy, Radiculopathy, Retinopathy // Thyroid Problems:

Musculoskeletal: WNL Weakness Amb Difficulty Limited Mobility/ROM Joint Pain/Stiffness Poor Balance Grip Strength R L Bed Bound   Chair Bound Contracture Paralysis

Has Assistive Device/s:

Needs DME:

ADL/IADLs: Activities Permitted: Bed Rest Cane Partial Weight Bearing Up as tolerated Walker Crutches Exercise Prescribed Wheelchair   Indep at Home Transfer bed<>chair   Other:

ADLs: Indep/Setup/Assist/Dep/Device Grooming Dress upper Dress Lower Bathing Toilet Transfer Toilet Hygiene Transfers Amb Eating

GG Scoring: 6 – Indep 5 – Setup 4 - Sup/touch 3 – Partial/Mod 2 – Substantial/Max 1 – Dep 7 –

Refused 9 – NA 10/88 - No attempt enviro/safety

GG Questions: Self Care Eating Oral Hygiene Shower Self Dress Upper Dress Lower Don/Doff Footwear

Mobility Roll Sit>Lying Lying>Sit Sit>Stand Chair<>Bed Toilet Transfer Car Transfer Walk 10 50 (+2 turns) 150   Steps 1 4 12 Pick up object WC Assist 50 150 (+2 turns)

A	**Nursing Diagnosis:**
	Possible New Medical Diagnosis (if any):
	Additional Notes:

P	**Nursing Intervention:**
	Consents/RS Signed: Y/N
	HHA Agency contact info given: Y/N
	Disciplines Needed: PT/OT/ST/SN/MSW, Aide
	Next Physician Visit:
	Pharmacy name and phone:

I also use a variation of the above comprehensive checklist which has been further simplified, to include just the basics. This shorter checklist serves as a simpler guide when visiting multiple patients and you have had more experience knowing what data can be gathered easily and which data may need more effort and attention to gather. It also fits into just one page.

Simple Checklist:

	Patient Name: Date: MD/DO: Reason for Visit: SOC, ROC, Recert, F/U, DC
S	**Recent hospitalization date (if any):** **Primary Dx:** Therapies pt receives at home: (IV, parenteral, NG, GT, O2, etc) Advanced directive – yes, no, DNR Pt Living Situation: (alone, w others,) **Medications (MED LIST):** **Allergies:** **Vaccines:** Flu, Pneumonia, Shingles, TB **PCG** name & contact:
O	*VITALS/PAIN – bp, hr, temp, rr, O2sat, *pain* Ht: Wt: BS: **SYSTEMS ASSESSMENT:** *eyes, ears, nose* *skin, pressure ulcer, wounds* **lung sounds**, *SOB, O2* *DM?, thyroid?* **Heart sound**, *rhythm, pulse, edema, pacemaker* *Last BM, GI probs, foley, ostomy, dials* *Diet, weight loss, eating well?*

	LOC, depression screen, sleeping well? *Mobility, DME needs, recent falls?*
A	Significant finding(s) to report:
P	**Nursing Intervention:** **Consents/RS Signed:** Y/N **HHA contact info given:** Y/N **Disciplines Needed:** PT/OT/ST/SN/MSW, Aide **Next Physician Visit:** **Pharmacy name and phone:**

Where to Download

To download either of these checklists, go to
OasisNinja.com/checklist

Chapter 9 - What is a SOAP NOTE - SOAP Notes for Physical Assessment

The SOAP note includes the subjective information from the patient. The introductory statement summarizes the patient's description and chief complaint, and fleshes out the components of the problem. Throughout the ages, the acronym OLD CARTS has been used as a guide for the most important questions to ask during an examination. The objective portion of the SOAP note is made up of Objective data. Listed below are some tips to help you develop a SOAP note:

Objective data

The objective data for SOAP physical assessment consists of several sections, each with a particular goal. First, the SOAP note should be based on a system and should reflect changes in the "S" and "O" of the patient over time, as well as changes in treatment or interim events. Second, the SOAP note should include a list of issues that the patient may have, along with their differential diagnoses and planned treatment.

The SOAP note is a medical record that allows healthcare professionals to make diagnoses and assess their patients. These notes contain subjective sections and objective data collected through physical means. In addition to the subjective section, SOAP notes also contain a section on the patient's lab tests, blood work, imaging, and diagnostics data. The assessment section includes the health professional's opinion. In addition, the note should document the patient's response to therapy.

The SOAP format is an essential form of communication between healthcare providers. It provides concise documentation of observations, data collected, and actions taken. The SOAP notes ensure proper credit for hard work. A few examples are listed below. However, the goal of SOAP notes is to capture the most important information and not waste time describing the least important. Soap notes also make it easier to read and scan documents. The use of standardized templates is also helpful for the standardization of the SOAP process and assessment methodology.

The SOAP note has two primary purposes: to document the health care encounter and to provide written proof of observations. First, it allows the healthcare provider to record data that they might not have gathered based on their observations. Second, it provides written evidence of the patient's condition. Finally, the SOAP note helps the health care provider determine the patient's needs and make the necessary changes. For both purposes, a SOAP note is useful and should be a valuable tool in the health care profession.

Subjective assessment

A SOAP note consists of the "S" and "O" components of the SOAP acronym. It should reflect the patient's change in the "S" and "O" over time as well as the response to any therapies and interim events. An SOAP note should be updated regularly to accurately portray the patient's current condition and any changes that may occur. During the course of the SOAP note, other information may be gathered such as the patient's risk factors, laboratory and radiology results, or outside consultation reports.

A patient's physical assessment notes should follow the SOAP framework, which describes the steps in a health care visit. During the subjective portion of the documentation, the patient should describe his or her symptoms and current feelings. This section should be written in the patient's own words, so it is essential to ensure the accuracy of the notes. Using quotation marks for direct quotes is also important. When writing notes, always make sure to include your patient's name, address, and insurance information.

The SOAP note is a useful method for documenting medical encounters. It streamlines medical professionals' note-taking by creating a system that stores client information in an organized fashion. The acronym stands for the four components of a SOAP note: subjective, objective, assessment, and plan. The SOAP note structure was originally developed by Larry Weed, an American physician, researcher, educator, and author. He used the SOAP note to track progress and evaluate a patient's condition.

The SOAP note begins with a subjective part, which includes subjective information that cannot be quantified. The next section focuses on the assessment process, which entails the diagnosis, the plan, and any additional tests that are needed. If the physician believes that the patient has a medical condition that needs to be treated, he will detail the findings in this section of the SOAP note. There are other parts of the SOAP note that may need further testing.

Most likely diagnosis

The most likely diagnosis of soap physical assessment (SOAP) note should include a differential diagnosis, active problems, the most likely diagnosis, and a less likely diagnosis. The diagnosis section should include evidence supporting the diagnosis, the patient's current status, the likelihood of improvement, and any complicating factors. The SOAP note should also explain the importance of the patient's treatment plan. If the diagnosis is not clear, it is essential to discuss the patient's symptoms and history to guide treatment.

The subjective part of the SOAP note contains information provided by the patient, such as the chief complaint or description. The SOAP note should be continually updated to reflect changes in the patient's condition over time. It should also include important risk factors, medication information, laboratory results, and outside consultation reports. During the SOAP note, the student must consider the most likely diagnosis and explain why. This section should be concise and informative.

A SOAP note is a form of medical note that records information from a patient's medical encounter. The information can come from the patient, a family member or friend, or from a study or database. The purpose of SOAP notes is to gather accurate information about the patient so that treatment and diagnosis can be effective.

Plan and Prognosis

The "S" and "O" components of a SOAP should be described in the notes. The diagnoses should be listed in descending order, starting with the most likely. Then, follow up with a list of possibilities that may not be as likely. Finally, the plan portion of the SOAP note should describe therapy and recommended tests and treatments. Finally, the patient's condition and risk factors must be discussed.

Notes from SOAP sessions should explain what the therapist did during the visit and how they managed it. For instance, if the patient has several major diagnoses, they should list each one. They should also specify whether they are stable or not. In addition, the notes should contain the differential diagnosis, or list two or three possible diagnoses. The SOAP note should also include the patient's next appointment and any homework that was given.

Notes from SOAPs are structured to increase the accuracy of the notes. They provide a systematic method for gathering all the information needed for proper diagnosis and treatment. The notes are organized to support the goal of providing the most effective care for the patient. In addition, SOAP notes focus on the Assessment, Plan, and History of Efficacy. They also provide a foundation for consultation with other care team members.

SECTION 2 – Before the Visit

Preparing to deal with people well in the home

Chapter 10 - The Three Phases of the Nurse-Client Relationship

In the nursing profession, establishing a nurse-client relationship involves several phases. According to Peplau, the nurse-client relationship consists of four phases that are sequential in nature. These phases are called the orientation, working, and termination phases. The orientation phase is the first. In this phase, the nurse introduces himself to the client and explains the purpose of the relationship. The nurse will ask the client about himself, his family, and the circumstances that brought him/her to the hospital. The nurse will also prepare the client for the termination phase of the relationship. The following are some of the stages in the nurse-client relationship.

Orientation Phase - Pre-interaction

The pre-interaction phases of the nurse-client relationships begin with the orientation phase, when both the nurse and client get acquainted with one another. The task of this phase is to build a relationship of trust and acceptance, set goals, and gather assessment information. Orientation also involves exploring feelings and expectations between the nurse and client. The working phase follows, where both the nurse and client work together to achieve the goals.

The first contact between nurse and client occurs in the pre-interaction phase, in which the novice nurse must explore his or her self. The first clinical experience in nursing can be stressful and challenging, and novice nurses are likely to bring misconceptions about the public and fears about themselves. New experiences lead to feelings of anxiety, ambivalence, and uncertainty, which are normal reactions to such an experience.

Introduction

An Introduction to the Nurse-Client Relationship begins with the introduction phase, which sets the tone for the whole relationship. This phase involves establishing rapport, communicating boundaries, explaining your role, and discussing your client's desired outcome. It also involves evaluating your own biases and the patient's condition. Identifying what the nurse can and cannot do can help you and the patient decide which therapeutic interventions to use.

A therapeutic nursing interaction can foster growth and insight, and the nurse and client work toward solutions that benefit both parties. Throughout the entire process, nurses must possess self-awareness and a philosophical belief. They must be patient-centered and nonjudgmental. A rapport-based relationship fosters a mutual trust and respect between the nurse and the client. The therapeutic relationship also promotes behavioral change.

Working phase

Once a client is comfortable with the nurse, the working phase involves identifying the client's problem, exploring solutions, and evaluating these solutions. The client's sense of security and safety is established, and the nurse and client develop an understanding of each other's roles and responsibilities. The working stage also includes the development of a positive self concept, communication, and assuming different roles. The nursing relationship can be challenging, but it's not impossible.

In the working phase of the nurse-client relationship, the nurses build rapport with their clients, establish their role, and collect data about their clients. At the same time, the nurses are collecting data on their clients, facilitating effective communication. The clients also learn about the nurse's role and their rights. After this phase, the relationship will move into the termination phase. It is critical that the nurse and the client agree on what their mutual goals are.

The working phase of the nurse-client relationship focuses on the process of establishing trust and addressing problems. Positive changes are common, but sometimes there is resistance and a lack of change. The nurse's role in the working phase of the nurse-client relationship is to promote change.

The nurse should identify the factors that contribute to a client's progress in the working phase. These include perceived attitudes of the nurse, the nature of the therapeutic sessions, and the things that happen between sessions. The working phase demonstrates supportive aspects of the relationship, whereas the ending phase involves mutual withdrawal. The client and the nurse have different perspectives on what constitutes a supportive relationship. The nursing role is to help the client establish a healthy balance between the two.

When the nurse and the patient complete their mutual goal, the working phase of the nurse-client relationship ends. The client and the nurse discuss changes in their health and their responses to these changes. They also discuss any emotional or physical responses to these changes. At the beginning of the working phase, the nurse establishes a rapport and trust. As the relationship progresses, the nurse attends to the physical health care needs of the client while developing solutions for the client's emotional and psychological needs.

The working phase of the nurse-client relationship involves identification of client problems, evaluating solutions, and applying these solutions to improve the client's quality of life. In the working stage, the nurse and client work to create a positive self-concept for each other and to promote coping mechanisms. The working stage also involves communication, establishing different roles, and exploring emotional feelings and responses.

The working phase of the nurse-client relationship focuses on building trust between the client and nurse.

The orientation phase involves establishing a climate of acceptance, trust, and contract between the nurse and the client. During this time, the nurse will explain his or her role, discuss the patient's expectations, and formulate nursing diagnoses. Lastly, the nurse and the client discuss their feelings and develop a problem-solving model. After the orientation phase, the working phase takes place, where the nurse and client work together to achieve the client's goal.

An Introduction to the Nurse-Client Relationship focuses on how nurses interact with patients, which is considered the core of nursing. The synthesis of theory describes the nurse-patient relationship as a bond of energy, a spiritual connection, and a living reality. A life-giving, compassionate, and meaningful nurse-patient relationship is one of the highest quality connections. Developing a life-giving relationship requires that both the patient and the nurse work together to help the patient and the nurse succeed in achieving their goals.

Throughout the patient-nurse interaction, nurses should maintain an open posture, demonstrating that they are receptive to the patient. A closed posture suggests a defensive posture. Leaning forward shows that the nurse is focused on the interaction and is interested in the client's needs. This shows that the nurse is focused and attentive. An open posture also shows that the nurse is genuinely interested in the client's interaction.

Implementation

In the implementation of the nurse-client relationship, nurses must first clarify the nature of the relationship. The client is at a crossroads because they may be distancing feelings from a past person. To counteract this, the nurse should help the client separate the past person from the present self. The priority nursing action should be to develop treatment goals, seek alternative placement, and explore thoughts about the client. This phase is particularly important if the patient feels sadness, dejection, or frustration.

During this phase, the nurse must build rapport with the client and create a comfortable and familiar situation. The nurse should then collect data about the patient's health and analyze the problem areas, plan interventions, and communicate expectations. The nurse and client may have difficulty setting goals or establishing trust. Once the nurse has established the basic framework, the relationship should evolve further. This phase is especially critical in mental health nursing. For example, the nurse should explain the nurse's role and the client should be aware of his or her rights and responsibilities.

The nurse-client relationship is the foundation of nursing practice. It is therapeutic in nature and focuses on the needs of the client. It requires the appropriate use of authority and respect, and abides by the standards of ethics. It must be accompanied by appropriate boundaries between professional and personal behavior. Further, it must ensure the client's dignity. A nurse must never be seductive or demeaning. If the nurse is engaging in inappropriate communication, it may not be a healthy environment.

In addition to building rapport with the client, the nurse should also establish boundaries between them and the nurse. It is essential to communicate the client's needs and role, establish boundaries, and adhere to them. The nurse-client relationship should be successful in all phases. The client's long-term health is the nurse's responsibility. A healthy and productive termination is vital to the success of the nurse-client relationship. There are also several guidelines that a nurse should follow when terminating the relationship.

Termination Phase

The final phase of the nurse-client relationship is known as the termination phase. This phase is the most important phase of the nurse-client relationship. It is the time when the nurse and patient exchange feelings, evaluate their progress toward the goals, and discuss the future of their relationship. This stage of the nurse-client relationship also involves evaluating the effectiveness of therapy and planning future meetings. During this phase, the nurse should monitor the patient's reactions and be able to handle the situation appropriately. If necessary, a supervisor should help if needed.

The termination phase is very important because you as the clinician do not want to be with the patient any longer than is necessary. Learning to terminate the interaction is key in managing your time as nurses tend to have many other things to do.

Chapter 11 - Therapeutic Communication - Improving Therapeutic Communication

If you want to improve your patient's safety and cooperation, you need to be more effective at therapeutic communication. Many times, ineffective communication can result in conflicting information, and patients may feel uncomfortable or apprehensive about certain things. The following tips can help you improve the quality of your communication with patients. By practicing these tips, you will be able to help patients cooperate more efficiently and safely with your treatments. Also, read on to learn more about the various aspects of therapeutic communication.

Ineffective therapeutic communication causes patients to feel apprehensive

Ineffective therapeutic communication is the root cause of the patient's apprehension during therapy sessions. A number of barriers to effective communication exist. These barriers include challenging and probing behaviors, changing the subject, and false reassurances. Other barriers include rejection, stereotyping, and judgments. The following are some ways to reduce the patient's apprehension during therapy sessions.

Effective therapeutic communication improves patient cooperation

Many nurses report that ineffective therapeutic communication can hinder the process of patient cooperation. While the patients themselves may not know the best methods of communication, nurses who know about these techniques will use them. Attitudes are a person's inclination to act in a certain way. Nurses who study the attitudes of their patients report that some patients know more about the process of nursing than others. Although this is not surprising, it is still surprising to find that the families of patients can be highly influenced by the communication style.

A nurse may use ineffective therapeutic communication if a patient is a new patient or a nervous patient. Anxiety also may delay therapeutic communication. Other barriers to patient cooperation include noise. Noise from other sources can interfere with any type of communication. Some patients turn on their radios while speaking. Nurses may chat on the telephone too much, which may also hinder effective communication. All these factors can impede patient cooperation.

Effective communication can help physicians deal with patients' anxiety and compliance with treatment. Effective communication may reduce patient anxiety and enhance patient compliance, resulting in a positive experience for all involved. For example, one patient refused to undergo catheterization despite his doctor's advice. The physician interpreted this behavior as a sign of ineffective communication and was able to persuade the patient to undergo the procedure. The patient's response was highly indicative of a doctor's communication skills.

A nurse who demonstrates effective therapeutic communication is likely to achieve many goals and benefit from the relationship between the nurse and patient. Ultimately, effective communication enhances patient cooperation by providing details of the patient's thoughts and feelings. For effective communication to occur, a nurse must foster rapport and trust with the patient. An effective rapport involves a mutual respect and trust, and the patient should feel comfortable discussing their personal concerns with the nurse.

Effective therapeutic communication improves patient safety

Ineffective therapeutic communication between clinicians can compromise patient safety. When the right information is not available to the right person at the right time, it can lead to inconsistent treatment plans, inadequate follow-up, medication errors, and increased polypharmacy. Ineffective communication is also associated with poor patient safety, a major concern for healthcare providers. The following table presents some possible explanations and implications for practice. While many factors are at play, some are common.

Lack of communication is a major source of patient safety problems. Hospitals often experience lengthy delays due to lack of communication between the staff. These delays lead to increased hospital stays, lower patient satisfaction scores, and increased costs.

Improving Communication Skills For Nurses

As a nurse, you must possess excellent communication skills. These include Active listening, Validation, and Honesty. In addition to these, you should be aware of the importance of active listening and teach-back. Several ways to improve your communication skills as a nurse are discussed below. Using the correct language can improve your patient care. If you have any problems or questions, please feel free to contact us. We will be happy to help.

Active listening

While a healthcare worker's job is to give full attention to a patient, they may find themselves distracted by their own thoughts and feelings. This distracting mental state affects the quality of care a patient receives. By actively listening, a health professional can absorb information more easily. This skill is a vital part of the nursing process, but it is a learned behavior. The best way to develop it is to practice it.

To practice active listening, nurses should ask patients for clarification when they are explaining something to them. The most effective way to do this is to ask broad opening questions that allow the patient to talk about whatever's on their mind. If a patient feels uncomfortable talking about their feelings, the nurse should encourage them with verbal and nonverbal cues, such as a nod or an eye contact. To encourage open communication, nurses can also offer general leads.

If a patient has a similar situation to one that they are experiencing now, nurses should encourage the patient to draw on this experience. Active listening allows patients to share information, develop empathy, and make comparisons. The nurse can record the conversation by asking open-ended questions and concluding by asking, "Does that sound right?"

Lastly, nurses should pay attention to patient comments. Patients respond to nonverbal cues when they are actively listening to what they're saying. For example, they might say something in a loud tone, but not have their body language catch it. They may respond more effectively with nonverbal cues, such as a slurred word. If a nurse understands what a patient is trying to say without interrupting them, they will be more effective in their nursing skills.

Validation

One of the most important tools nurses can use is validation. When people feel that their feelings and requests are being heard and understood, their well-being increases. Nurses who use validation to express their needs can strengthen their relationship with patients and their families. By acknowledging someone's needs, they will be able to more effectively respond to requests and improve patient care. It is also an empowering tool for family-centered communication and can help all parties feel heard.

A self-efficacy scale for communication skills is a helpful tool for evaluating these skills. It can also be used to create institutional strategies for effective communication. In this study, the Spanish version of the Self-efficacy questionnaire-12 in communication skills was validated as a valid and reliable instrument. Further, it is essential for the validation of communication skills for nurses. The results of the study are discussed in the following paragraphs.

In the course of patient communication, it is important for nurses to understand the perspective, beliefs, and perspectives of the person they are talking to. For example, nurses must determine if the patient's nonverbal expressions are indicative of pain or disgust. As a result, nurses should be sure to clarify the meaning of every nonverbal gesture. In addition to this, nurses must learn to read the body language of their patients.

A nurse's interpersonal communication skills can significantly affect the quality of interventions in different care services. Nurses who can listen to a patient and validate their feelings and opinions are more likely to build trust with their patients. This, in turn, increases the quality of decisions, patient motivation, and clinical outcomes. Therefore, nurses must learn to listen to others in order to be an effective communicator. This skill is particularly important when dealing with patients and their families.

Validation is an important part of communication

A key part of effective communication is validating the perspectives of your clients. This includes understanding how your clients view issues and their own experiences. Then, you can understand how cultural differences can challenge health professionals and service users. Understanding how to properly validate someone's experiences and views can help you build better rapport with patients, families, and colleagues. Here are four examples of validating other people. Identifying your clients' values, beliefs, and perspectives will help you understand how to best address their needs and concerns.

Communicating effectively requires accurate assessment of the individual's beliefs, values, perspectives, and perceptions. Nurses must also consider the recipient's nonverbal cues. Nonverbal grimacing, for example, is a signal that the receiver is in pain or disgust. A skilled nurse will be able to interpret nonverbal cues and determine what is being communicated.

When interpreting a patient's language and body language, nurses must ask their patient if their understanding is correct. Many misunderstandings arise when people fail to check the meaning of words. When delivering an explanation, the nurse should ask for confirmation from the patient. Similarly, eye contact and the position of the body should be consistent. Verbal responses should be regular and encouraging, and the response should show that the nurse understands the facts and emotions expressed by the patient.

Nurses who develop critical thinking and self-examination are the best communicators. Nurses with this skill are able to integrate theoretical knowledge about communication into their practice and evaluate the effects of their actions. They can also be effective communicators by developing their creative and critical thinking skills. This is a critical skill to have if you want to improve your communication skills. All this will help you become a better nurse.

Honesty

Effective communication is essential for nurses to build rapport with patients and solicit important health information. Effective communication among members of the healthcare team also ensures a smooth patient journey. In a busy clinical workday, it is easy to get lost in the shuffle, and when a healthcare worker comes across as uninterested or cold, they may endanger the patient-provider relationship. To avoid these problems, nurses should adopt a positive self-image and practice openness.

In end-of-life care, good communication skills are especially critical. Oftentimes, patients and caregivers are uncomfortable with words such as "death." They may be afraid that by being honest, they will be betraying hope. However, honesty allows them to explore alternative possibilities and even talk about "a good death."

Nursing professionals must establish trust with patients by being honest and respectful in their conversations. Regardless of their role, nurses should always face their patients and communicate with them on the same eye level. This way, they convey mutuality, equality, and a position of power. The patient will also be more likely to be open to listening to their nurse when they are able to feel comfortable and relaxed. Also, nurses must establish trust by introducing themselves and letting patients know they can talk to anyone.

In addition to oral communication, nurses must be able to understand the needs of their clients through written correspondence. Nurses should be able to write clearly, as they will be able to share important information with their patients. In addition to writing clearly, nurses should be able to speak with patients in a manner that is clear and professional. They should also be able to use medical terminology and abbreviations correctly.

Avoiding harmful silence

There are several factors that contribute to the issue of avoiding silence when communicating with nurses. Several studies have shown that nurses often fail to communicate when they have a problem, and this silence can have adverse effects on the health of patients. In addition to health-related quality, the problem can also affect patient safety. If you notice that the silence in your department is affecting patient care, consider how you can improve the situation by addressing the root cause of the issue.

When two parties lack common ground, conflict results. Though conflict is necessary and often offers an opportunity to express different perspectives and values, it can become an impediment to communication. Moreover, it can detract from the task or purpose being carried out. Nurses often strive to achieve collaborative relationships with patients, families, and colleagues. However, they often feel unable to accomplish this goal if they cannot communicate effectively with others.

One way to overcome this dilemma is to practice active listening. It involves showing interest in the patient and engaging with them throughout the conversation. By offering general leads during the conversation, the nurse can propel the discussion. Using silence can also give both the nurse and the patient time to think and broach new topics. This technique is particularly helpful in patient care. But remember that there are times when silence is necessary. If the silence is too long or uncomfortable, the patient may feel unwelcome, and the nursing staff will be unable to help them.

When you are speaking with patients, be sure to maintain eye contact with them and avoid defensive posture. Make sure to maintain eye contact with them, so that they feel that you are communicating with them on a level that is respectful to both of you. You should also maintain an open posture, which conveys equality and mutuality. It is also important to avoid a defensive posture because it can cause confusion in interpreting what the other person is saying.

Using Silence As Therapeutic Communication

Silence as a therapeutic communication tool can be beneficial in many counseling sessions. Intentional silence can help counsellors process material from clients. This is an excellent way to facilitate reflection or reassurance, as well as to facilitate a natural end to the session. Silence allows counselors to process client material without paraphrasing or giving advice. The silence can also help counsellors process material and understand the client's material more clearly.

Chapter 12 - Importance of Active Listening

It is not just a good way to reduce conflict in the workplace, but also a great way to improve patient interaction. Active listening is essential in the nurse-client relationship, as it will allow you to gain clarity about the subject you are discussing and helps you gather the data you need.

Improves communication

Active listening is one of the most important techniques to use when interacting with others. It is the foundation of effective communication, and is essential in resolving conflicts and solving problems. Practicing active listening can help you improve your relationships and career. Active listeners do not interrupt other people and maintain eye contact and positive body language. If you are a passive listener, you may even look away, but this does not convey a positive message.

While active listening is not an exact science, it can be a highly effective tool in fostering trust and empathy. It requires a focus on the speaker's words, and not just scanning their body language for cues. Active listeners are also focused on the speaker and engage with nonverbal cues, like eye contact and nodding. This ensures the other person feels that the other person is paying attention and retaining information.

Active listening is the process of paying attention to the speaker's words and body language. The listener refrains from interjecting, despite the lapse of time in which silence occurs. They also convey clear signs that they are paying attention to what the speaker is saying and refrain from offering their own opinions and solutions. These signals include nods, eye contact, and simple utterances. These signs indicate that active listening is a key part of good communication.

Active listening helps build trust. When people feel they have trust in you, they are more likely to cooperate with you. Active listening allows you to hear different perspectives, which helps prevent misunderstandings. Developing trust with team members is essential for healthy working relationships. When you use this technique, you will be more successful in your business and caring for patients. And the results are immediate. You'll have more trust, more empathy, and better communication.

Reduces conflict

The importance of active listening cannot be overstated. Most conflicts are caused by misunderstandings. Not listening to instructions can cause hardships for yourself. In addition to creating an unhealthy work environment, not listening to instructions may also sabotage the relationship between coworkers and not just with patients. Instead of trying to resolve conflicts, try listening first and then responding with compassion. Active listening is a powerful tool that will improve your career.

Another way to resolve conflict is by tracking conflicts. By tracking conflicts in a journal, nurses can learn how to effectively handle them when they happen. They can discuss their observations with others, and this will prepare them for future conflict resolution situations. While you are practicing active listening, try to make sure you do not interrupt other people, as this may lead to confusion and further conflict. Also, remember to repeat back what you have heard in your own words.

When you practice active listening, you will find it easier to understand what others are saying. This will make you more comfortable with the other party. While it may be difficult to keep silence during a heated discussion, active listening helps build understanding and a sense of partnership. Moreover, it will reduce conflict and improve the quality of work product. Active listening will make your team more productive and happy. But what is more important, it can also save you time.

While some conflicts may not have winners or losers, most of them are actually reflections of real disagreements about how a particular organization should function. In these cases, the parties involved acknowledge that a problem exists and agree to address it. When this happens, they try to understand each other's point of view and try to recognize how the situation changed. If they are unable to resolve the conflict themselves, they can engage in a third party, such as a mediator.

Listen to Learn

Active listening helps you remember new information. It helps you recall the specific details and understand new topics. This is essential when you're passing along messages, training, or instructions to your team or patients. Active listening also allows you to summarize the key points of what the speaker has to say without ignoring the other person. It also gives the speaker the chance to clarify. While listening, make sure you're not preoccupied with other things.

Active listening also helps in reducing workplace conflict. Most conflicts in the workplace stem from misunderstandings. Not listening to what others have to say will result in hardship for yourself and others. It can also make patients or coworkers angry, which can create an unproductive and hostile atmosphere. Active listening will help you develop effective retention strategies and boost employee morale. A company that values its employees will keep them for a long time.

Reduces workplace distractions

There is a growing body of evidence that active listening helps to reduce workplace distractions. Studies have found that an average person's mind wanders 47% of the time. To increase effective listening skills, employees should learn to put down their cell phones, tablets, and other electronic devices and focus on the other person's needs. In addition to being an excellent way to improve communication, active listening can increase productivity, decrease stress, and improve morale.

Active listening involves focusing on the speaker's words and ideas. It requires complete attention, ensuring that the message is understood and responded to thoughtfully. In contrast to passive listening, active listening ensures that the listener engages with the speaker and recalls specific details without repeating information. Active listening also ensures that the person who is speaking is fully understood and that he or she is able to respond appropriately.

By listening, people will feel more valued and comfortable sharing information with you. This will create a more productive environment. Those who practice active listening will be more likely to collaborate with one another and take part in projects. This will reduce conflicts and boost morale in the workplace. Active listening also helps prevent misunderstandings. This will help to make communication easier, more efficient, and create a more congenial relationship with employees.

Practice Makes Perfect

While learning how to listen, you can practice active listening skills with partners or small groups. When listening to a person, refrain from interrupting or making judgmental comments, and ask questions if needed. Active listening is the key to deep conversations. By respecting silence, you can create an environment in which students are comfortable sharing their opinions. Active listening skills also foster positive emotional states.

In addition to improving communication skills, active listening can help people learn to respond with empathy and compassion. Empathic listeners are good at initiating conversations, but this doesn't mean you have to fix a problem for them. The process of listening helps people develop their emotional intelligence, because most people do not want to talk about their problems - they just want to express their frustration. Listening to a person's thoughts can give you insight into the problem they're having and can help you come up with a solution.

Chapter 13 - How to Use Silence Effectively - Intentional Silence

Intentional silence is an effective form of therapeutic communication. If you find yourself unable to say anything to your client, it can be helpful to let them be without interruption. It can be more effective than mindless talking, since silence gives you the opportunity to reflect on your thoughts and the situation. Often times, silence allows you to focus on the situation at hand. Here are a few reasons why intentional silence can be therapeutically beneficial.

Intentional silence serves as a form of punctuation during patient interactions. When it occurs, the client can process what is said and move on to other material. It also gives the client time to make connections. Moreover, silence can be a very useful tool for helping a client put names to their feelings. The benefits of silence as therapeutic communication can be profound. You should use it whenever appropriate, and avoid leading the client into a conversation.

Silence is an important part of a therapeutic relationship, and can promote growth. As long as you are aware of your presence and remain calm, this form of silence can help your patient process health changes. It also provides the opportunity for your patient to process their feelings and reflect on their condition. For the clinician, this type of therapy is an excellent tool to help their patient express their emotions and deal with stress. A nurse can bring silence to the client's attention and then make it part of the therapeutic process.

The benefits of intentional silence as therapeutic communication are immense. It helps a patient to think about the next topic. It gives them the chance to reflect on their situation and their own feelings. As a result, it can be effective in forming deeper positive relationships. It's important to keep in mind that silence can be a powerful tool in psychodynamic therapy. If you're interested in learning more about intentional silence as a form of therapeutic communication, consider reading this article.

The process of using silence in group therapy is similar to that of individual therapy. It gives clients a space to practice mindfulness. It also allows the client to reflect on his or her own feelings and to clarify their own. As a result, silence in group therapy may be a good way to create an environment where people feel comfortable, safe, and relaxed. If a group is unable to communicate with each other, they will not be able to reach a productive solution.

Open-ended questions

Silence as therapeutic communication and open-ended question techniques are two methods for communicating with patients in your care. Open-ended questions encourage more detailed answers than closed-ended ones, and they foster greater information about the patient's emotions, thoughts, and behaviors. They also facilitate more open ventilation, which is critical for patients undergoing mechanical ventilation or intubation. However, open-ended questions are not enough. To be effective, nurses should be aware of when to use closed and open-ended questions.

Using open-ended questions allows you to continue the conversation. You can ask a follow-up question if necessary, so that the other party has ample opportunity to expand on the topic at hand. This method of open-ended questioning is highly recommended for facilitating the therapeutic process, as it allows the speaker to reveal more information about themselves. It also encourages the other person to elaborate on their responses, which in turn enables you to get a deeper understanding of their concerns and ideas.

The best way to encourage open-ended questions is to listen closely to what the patient says. You should be mindful of how often you use closed-ended questions, as they may seem like manipulation. If you frequently ask open-ended questions, you can switch the communication approach and get more information out of your patients. You can even use a simple prompt to help your patient get started with an open-ended question.

If you want to improve your patient's quality of life, use open-ended questions and silence as a means to communicate. Remember that open-ended questions require the patient to make more effort than closed-ended questions. Using open-ended questions can help you better understand your patient's feelings and needs, and make it easier for you to provide them with the highest quality of care. So, practice what you're taught!

Reflection

One method for therapeutic communication involves using reflection to elicit a response. The speaker may not feel the need to respond directly, but reflective responses can help the speaker focus his or her thoughts and words. This can be a very helpful tool if the speaker is feeling frustrated, angry, or otherwise struggling to express himself or herself. Using reflection can be as simple as mirroring what the speaker says. In doing so, the speaker feels heard and can continue speaking.

Nurses who use reflective techniques may ask patients for their input on certain issues. The purpose of this approach is to encourage thoughtfulness in the patient and to encourage autonomy. Reflection has a number of positive effects. In addition to encouraging thoughtfulness, it can also encourage the patient to take control of their healthcare. In addition to encouraging thoughtfulness, reflective communication helps the nurse to provide a patient with a sense of peace and comfort.

A skilled listener can use reflection to gauge a speaker's feelings. Reflection is a way to increase a client's awareness of emotions and to label them. When a counselor has a varied emotional vocabulary, they can tailor the words they use to match the experience of the client. Reflection is a basic, yet effective, therapeutic communication technique. There are three main types of reflection. One is active, another is passive.

Several other studies have used reflection to promote healing. The most commonly used model is the role-play-based method. This method emphasizes the fundamental principles of the four psychotherapeutic perspectives. It allows the student to use more than one perspective to enhance their understanding of each of these. The author of this article used the model to train student therapists. The first author role-played the patient, and the second author role-played the patient and other members of the patient's social network.

One key to implementing therapeutic communication is identifying barriers. When barriers come up, it's important to recognize them and work on overcoming them. Rewarding patient's efforts is a vital part of establishing therapeutic communication. But remember that each patient is unique, so it's important not to compare what they have achieved with what you have done. The patient is the center of the therapy. It's essential for the nurse to acknowledge their individuality and to incorporate their preferences.

Humor

Using humor as a form of therapeutic communication requires tact and creativity. Knowing when to use humor is the first step to using it effectively. Humor isn't the best choice when a patient has just been diagnosed with a devastating disease. It is most effective when patients need information to help them make sense of new medications or side effects. But it's also important to know when to use humor in your clinical settings.

Using humor in clinical settings has numerous benefits, including helping nurses deal with patients' challenging behaviors. It also creates a bond between patients and nurses, and can decrease feelings of depression, anxiety, and embarrassment. Using humor is a therapeutic communication technique that can be planned or spontaneous, but can have lasting benefits.

Chapter 14 - Nontherapeutic Communication - What to Avoid

There are many types of nontherapeutic communication techniques including False Reassurances, Overloading, and Judging. These can be harmful, as they suggest that the nurse knows best. Instead, therapeutic communication techniques should focus on asking good questions, guiding, and listening to the patient's needs.

False Reassurances

There are many nontherapeutic communication techniques, but one technique is particularly harmful. False Reassurances are statements that the nurse makes without being able to verify them. An example is a nurse's statement to an inmate about an HIV test: "Don't worry, it will be fine." While the nurse is trying to be helpful, this false reassurance actually devalues the client's experience. Instead of reassurance, the nurse may try to assess the client by making observations and verbalizing what they have observed. The nurse may also try to encourage the patient to recognize certain behaviors and make comparisons with the nurse's perceptions.

When a patient asks for help, the nurse may ask what they think should be done. Reflection is a positive therapeutic communication technique, which helps the patient take responsibility for their own healthcare decisions and teaches them that their opinions are important. The nurse must remember that patients are the center of their own care and should be given enough time to ask questions and perform tasks. False Reassurances undermine the importance of therapeutic communication.

Another example of a false reassurance is the nurse's assurance that the patient will get better. The nurse may feel better by reassurance, but this does not guarantee the patient's success. False reassurances also block expression and make the client feel uncomfortable. For this reason, the nurse must be careful and never use false reassurances in nontherapeutic communication techniques.

Judging

There are a few common communication mistakes that can lead to poor patient-provider relationships: judgement and approval. Avoid using the words "you should" or "don't." When giving advice or addressing a personal issue, avoid starting the conversation with "you should." Changing the subject is a common communication mistake, but it actually blocks the flow of communication and can discourage the patient from sharing in the future.

Stereotyping

One of the worst things nurses can do is engage in stereotyping. It impedes effective communication and inhibits the nurturing of interpersonal relationships with patients. Effective communication is crucial for nursing, and all nurses should aim to become proficient in therapeutic engagement.

Instead use reflection: When a patient is having a difficult time talking about their symptoms, they may turn to their caregiver for advice. In this case, reflection can be a positive therapeutic communication technique. The healthcare professional can ask the patient what he or she believes should be done and encourages autonomy. In addition, reflection is a method of expressing gratitude for the patient's trust and support.

Overloading

Overloading a patient is an example of a nontherapeutic communication technique. The patient may ask a nurse for advice regarding a problem or concern, or they may simply want to talk about a problem they are having. Reframing the patient's perspective on the situation can promote autonomy and encourage them to take responsibility for their health. This technique can be helpful in addressing many aspects of a patient's care.

When a patient tells a story or makes an important decision about the condition, a nurse can acknowledge that statement and rephrase it as a question. The patient's statement is then a prompt for patient education. This technique requires the nurse to listen carefully and determine if their impression matches the statement. Then, the nurse can ask the question based on their impression. Once the patient has rephrased it, the nurse can then use it to make the patient more comfortable about talking about their problem.

When therapeutic communication techniques fail, barriers exist. The patient is unable to understand or follow an effective care plan, or the nurse is not able to develop a trusting nurse-patient relationship. Both problems can affect patient outcomes, so it is important to be aware of any barriers and try to solve them before they become overwhelming. However, it's important to remember that communication is a two-way street and should be handled with respect, even if the patient can't speak out.

Incongruence

In therapeutic communication, there is an incongruence between what the client says and what he or she knows. Congruence between client and therapist is important, as therapists are personally invested in the therapeutic relationship and may draw on their own experiences to foster the relationship. A therapist's unconditional positive regard facilitates increased self-regard in the client and increased awareness of distorted self-worth.

Invalidation

While many well-intentioned individuals may claim to be validators, their actions can be detrimental to the other person. Invalidation is the opposite of acceptance and nurture, and it can create a negative emotional impact on the other person. Often, invalidating messages are used to make someone feel crazy or unreal. Here are some ways invalidating messages can affect a relationship:

Reflection is a technique that is positive in therapeutic communication. It involves asking a patient what they think should be done in a specific situation. Invalid questions are often those that are irrelevant to the patient's medical history. A nurse should never ask a question just to satisfy her own curiosity. The patient needs to feel empowered to make decisions about their healthcare, and reflection is a great way to do this.

It is important to understand how nontherapeutic communication techniques can negatively impact the patient. Nontherapeutic communication techniques can impede patient expression, impair the nurse-client relationship, and negatively affect nursing interventions.

The patient interview is an essential component of nursing assessment. During this time, the nurse must learn all the information she needs to get a complete patient history through proper therapeutic communication so the patient trusts the nurse and the nurse can gather all the data they need to do their job well.

Chapter 15 - Stress Management for Nurses

Many factors can contribute to effective stress management for nurses. One of these factors is the role of friends and family members. In order to overcome stress, nurses should have the support of superiors, family members, and friends. An effective context for support can be created by authorities, such as providing adequate equipment, positive feedback, and continuing educational workshops. Additionally, effective communication skills and access to counselors can also aid in stress management. Positive outcomes of stress management include an understanding of the meaning of life and personal growth.

Relaxation stations

Students learn how to cope with stress and use useful strategies in a classroom center setting by using a Relaxation Station. Students learn to practice stress-management skills and personal health habits, which they later use in the workplace. They also learn how to set up a relaxation station, complete with supplies and a rubric. Students use the stations as a form of personal stress relief, communicating the strategies they are using to their peers or an adult.

Researchers at UCF have found that relaxing the mind and body can reduce stress levels. Nurses who practice progressive muscle relaxation can identify when they are becoming tense and destress their bodies. The practice may help reduce the negative effects of the pandemic. The researchers also found that nurses with a higher stress level were more likely to report poor quality sleep. They hope to further evaluate the effectiveness of relaxation techniques to reduce stress levels in nursing.

Hospitals and nursing facilities are experimenting with various ways to relieve stress and improve employee satisfaction. Some of these methods include creating serenity rooms with soft lighting, comfortable chairs, relaxing music, and pleasing artwork. Creating a calming environment for staff can lead to improved health, increased job satisfaction, and even better care. Hospitals can create a stress-reduction environment in breakrooms by installing such a station.

Yoga

A recent study of nurses exposed to high levels of stress found that participants who practiced yoga regularly reported a reduction in work-related stress. The researchers compared participants' scores on the Pittsburgh Quality Index and a questionnaire measuring work-related stress and sleep. They found that both measures were significantly improved when participants practiced yoga, even when they weren't in an intensive care unit. Yoga is a complementary treatment for stress that improves health by reducing anxiety, depression, and back pain.

Recent studies of nurses have shown that yoga has beneficial effects on nurses' mental health and physical well-being, and it also helps nurses develop self-care. While previous studies have focused on nurse-specific outcomes, the results of this study show promising results. Yoga can promote emotional resilience, reduce stress, and increase clinical decision making. Despite the promising effects of yoga, further research is needed to determine the best way to implement it into a nursing practice.

Several interventions have been implemented to help healthcare workers reduce their stress and improve their overall well-being. These interventions include rescheduling shifts and increasing the frequency and duration of breaks. In addition to yoga, the study of healthcare workers also revealed that meditative practices such as mindfulness and breathing exercises improve psycho-physical well-being. The results showed that nurses who practiced yoga showed significantly fewer symptoms of physical exhaustion and a higher level of self-care and self-awareness.

The meditative and physical components of yoga are especially beneficial for busy nurse moms. The techniques of yoga can improve concentration, create inner peace, and cultivate compassion. All of these benefits are great for the health and wellbeing of nurses. You can even incorporate a daily yoga practice into your schedule if you're a busy nurse! You'll be glad you did! It might even make a difference in the quality of your work.

Meditation

The benefits of meditation for nurses are numerous. The practice helps nurses relax and manage their stress levels. In addition to relaxing the mind, many meditation techniques can be performed anywhere, even at work. Smartphone applications make it easy for nurses to meditate without the distraction of their office or home. Meditation helps to calm the mind and clear away unimportant information, thus calming the jumbled stream of consciousness. In addition to helping nurses deal with the stresses of their jobs, it also helps them reduce depression and insomnia.

Mindfulness meditation teaches nurses to pay attention to the present moment. This is crucial for nurses, who must be constantly on their toes. They need to remain focused and grounded in order to be able to respond appropriately to stressful situations. Through meditation, nurses can learn how to cultivate their inner thoughts and develop self-compassion. This is key to managing stress in today's complex health care environment. Further research into the benefits of meditation for nurses is needed to prove its effectiveness in this field.

The study used a 204-bed community hospital as an example. Its holistic care approach has been growing in the last couple of years. It includes a policy-guided holistic care council, a shared governance structure, aromatherapy, and massage chairs in the nursing breakrooms. The researchers believe that these practices are beneficial for nurses, especially those who work in an environment of high stress and high anxiety. They also note that this technique may help reduce the risk of chronic diseases like heart disease and high blood pressure.

When you need help, talk to your manager about your concerns and the ways in which you can alleviate your stress. Nurses who have a high-level of stress should seek support from their supervisor or colleagues, and they should feel free to share their feelings with others. These people are the ones who can help them make decisions that will help them feel more positive and reduce their overall stress. So, why wait any longer to try meditation for stress management?

Talking to coworkers

Nurses can often find it difficult to deal with the stresses of the job. However, talking with coworkers can help ease this burden. It is helpful to try to understand the root cause of the stress, as it will allow you to offer the most practical solutions and tactics. The most common causes of stress include too much work, uncertainty about how to succeed, and interpersonal conflicts. If you can identify the source of the stress, you can help your coworker find practical solutions and tactics to reduce the effects of the stressful event.

Nursing stress is caused by a variety of factors. For example, conflict with coworkers and management can increase anxiety levels. Taking notice of the triggers will allow you to prepare for them and lessen their effect on your health. For example, you may find that you have a hard day at work because of poor staffing. In that case, the solution may lie in improving the communication between the manager and the staff.

In addition to talking to colleagues, nurses can discuss their own stress levels and their own health. In addition, they should share their successes with their coworkers and be willing to open up about their experiences of stress. Talking to coworkers can be extremely helpful in reducing stress and making the work environment a healthier place for nurses. By being transparent and open with colleagues, nurses can ensure that they have an effective stress management system.

The Lazarus and Folkman theory focuses on two types of coping strategies for nurses. This model identifies three general scenarios and a list of possible stressors. These patterns of coping result in the gray outcome, which is the prevailing response of nurses to a stressful situation. It is important to note that nurses adopt a variety of strategies for managing stress, including those based on self-reliance, situational control, and spiritual coping.

Creating a safe environment

Nurses in high-stress work environments face a high risk of developing depression and anxiety. Moreover, they may experience ongoing feelings of lethargy, fatigue, and depression. Stress management strategies can help nurses improve their overall health and maintain vitality in their roles. Nurse leaders and educators can also play a role in stress management for nurses by providing resources and information on self-care strategies. Following are some practical tips to support nurse stress management.

Creating a safe environment for nurse stress management requires a focus on clinician well-being. Stress can affect patient safety and prevent employees from delivering innovative and safe care. In addition to increasing the risk of errors, it also inhibits open communication and impedes communication among workers who know the system best. Therefore, hospitals must recognize the impact of workplace stress on their workforce to improve patient care. And in order to reduce the risk of errors and other factors related to patient care, they should expand the availability of confidential mental health services.

The first step in stress management for nurses is understanding the importance of self-care and accepting the fact that they need to protect their own health to perform their jobs well. Creating a safe environment for nurses will enable them to reap the benefits of their profession: a broader perspective on life and the ability to help others in times of crisis; increased tolerance and gratitude for others; and a greater appreciation for family and friends.

Healthcare institutions can play a role in promoting healthy living environments for nurses. By encouraging nurses to practice mindfulness, healthcare organizations can help them develop healthy lifestyle patterns and combat stressful working environments. In addition to developing a safe environment for nurses, agencies can also promote stress management programs for employees. For example, they can offer aromatherapy and support rounds to reduce workplace stress. A quiet room with candles and herbal tea is also an excellent resource.

Social support

Building a strong social network is essential for reducing the effects of stress on your physical and psychological health. Research has shown that social support can mitigate genetic vulnerability and confer resilience to stress. It may affect the HPA and noradrenergic systems, and may influence central oxytocin pathways. However, more research is needed to find specific interventions to improve social support. In the meantime, you can start making friends and improve relationships to increase the amount of social support you have in your life.

When establishing a social network for stress management, make sure it is a place where you feel comfortable. You should feel comfortable with the beliefs, practices, and expectations of the people with whom you associate. You should not be expected to agree with every individual in the group. It should be a place where you feel accepted, peaceful, and energized. However, you should avoid being around people who are negative or coercive.

Having a close network of people is a lifesaver. Studies have shown that individuals with a rich social network are less likely to engage in risky behaviors, avoid negative appraisals, and adhere to treatment. In addition, individuals with a rich social network are believed to engage in active coping mechanisms. Among cardiac patients, high levels of social support are associated with lower rates of depression. And, it may even help patients recover more quickly from cardiovascular events.

The study also revealed that individuals with a larger network of support and mentors are more likely to successfully manage their stress. However, the study's findings do not support a causal relationship between social support and depressive symptoms. While this study does not support the theory of social support as a treatment for depression, it does support the concept of "social buffering" and the stabilizing or regulatory effect of social support on the HPA axis.

Exercise

There are many benefits of exercise for stress management. Not only does exercise decrease stress, but it is also good for your health. You will notice a decrease in overall stress response when you exercise, as well as a boost in mental clarity and a healthy body. There are also many additional benefits of exercise, such as improved brain function. Here are some of the most common benefits of exercise. You'll notice a dramatic improvement in your health in no time!

Physical activity is a proven stress-buster. People who enjoy physical activity will stick with it for the long term. Generally, exercise for stress management involves doing a certain activity more than once a week, with a break-in period of around five to six sessions. Exercises should focus on body movement, muscular endurance, agility, coordination, and accuracy. General fitness includes endurance, strength, balance, flexibility, and agility.

Physical activity improves your overall self-esteem. Physical activity also improves your body's ability to use oxygen. It can also help you shed body fat, a common problem among overweight people. Exercise is also a useful part of a weight-loss programme. However, exercise will not solve the root cause of your stress, such as an impending deadline. You might be better off finding a new hobby that will help you relax and de-stress, or spending more time with family and friends.

In addition to its physical benefits, exercise for stress management also improves your mental well-being. Whether you're a savvy weight lifter or a regular attendee of a high-intensity interval training class, there's something for everyone. Try taking a walk around your neighborhood to reduce your stress level. This will improve your mood and give you a renewed energy. Even a simple brisk walk will increase your energy levels, and you'll feel healthier afterward.

Chapter 16 - Time Management For Nurses - Effective Use of Time

How Time Management Can Help You Get More Done in Less Time

Learning effective time management can help you get more done while managing stress at the same time. Time management is the conscious use of time to achieve your goals. Incorporating strategies to maximize your time helps you get more done in less time. These strategies include setting goals and prioritizing tasks. You can automate recurring tasks to free up time. And if you're really ambitious, you can even use a time management program to get things done even faster.

Setting goals

One of the best ways to improve your time management skills is to set specific goals for your work. This will prevent you from wasting time by wondering what tasks need to be done next. It will also help you avoid getting distracted and working on unimportant tasks. A proper goal should have a deadline. This will help you manage time and focus on important tasks. Your team will also benefit from setting goals.

First, you need to write down your goal. Set a timeframe for each goal and write them down. Then, set a series of smaller goals that will help you reach your main goal. Try to arrange them as an organizational chart. After you've written them down, prioritize them and start the process of achieving them. Writing down your goals makes the process of achieving them much easier. Then, make a list of smaller goals and priorities.

Set clear goals for every event in the week. Once he has mastered the art of setting goals, you can move on to improving your time management skills. This may take some time, but it will eventually pay off. It's important to create realistic goals.

Prioritizing tasks

A key part of effective time management is knowing your priorities. A simple list of all tasks is not effective. List important tasks first, then urgent ones. This will help you avoid wasting time and energy on unimportant tasks. Then, list tasks based on length, importance, urgency, and reward. You can also divide tasks into categories based on their importance, urgency, and length. When creating a list, make sure to include both personal and work-related tasks.

To find out the highest priority tasks, prioritize them by asking yourself, "Who will be impacted by this?"

To determine which tasks are most important, write down the results of these activities. Then, prioritize those that will have the biggest impact on the results of the team. Think of the ROI of each activity. If a task is a small contribution, it may be worth doing after all. However, if you feel like you can't complete a task in time, use a to-do list instead. The benefits of making lists are many.

If you are a busy person, having a system for prioritizing tasks is an essential skill for effective time management. The more you know about prioritization, the more likely you will be productive.

Automating recurring tasks

You can save time by automating recurring tasks. For example, if you have to clean out your refrigerator every week, you can set it to come to your door at 7 a.m. You can also set reminders for recurring tasks to pop up at a specific time every week. Once you have created an automated task, you can set it to appear on your calendar, so you don't have to worry about forgetting it.

There are many benefits to automating repetitive tasks. Not only do you get rid of the time you spend doing these tasks, but you also reduce the possibility of human error. You can choose to automate simple tasks, or go a step further and use complex automated tools to do all your work. Regardless of whether you are automating a daily task or a one-time job, it will free up valuable time and help you improve your productivity.

You can use various programs to automate recurring tasks in Notion. Bardeen, for example, is free and easy to use. This time management solution does not require any programming knowledge. It requires only a Notion database, which most people already have. If not, you can duplicate it in the Notion Automation Hub. In both cases, you can set up the recurring tasks you want. You can then follow the instructions on the software.

Focusing on one task at a time

If you want to maximize your productivity and time management skills, focus on one task at a single time. By eliminating the need to jump from task to task, you'll be able to get more done in less time. And because you'll be focusing on one task at a time, you'll be able to manage your workload more effectively. Besides, it will reduce the number of urgent tasks you have to handle.

Another tip for time management is to set aside dedicated blocks of time for each task. This is also called focus time. This time can be dedicated to specific tasks, which will help you achieve quality results. You can use focus time for any kind of work, including the most important ones, such as writing and researching. If you're able to set aside specific blocks of time for focus time each day, you'll be able to achieve your goals in a shorter amount of time.

Research has shown that when you focus on one task at a time, you're more productive than when you multitask. According to Harvard psychologists, people spend 47% of their waking time multitasking. That's like texting while driving! Multitasking is a vicious cycle. Once started, it's difficult to stop. Multitasking also tends to self-multiply, meaning that more work is needed to achieve the same result. By focusing on one task at a time, you'll be able to break this cycle.

Keeping a To-do list

Keeping a to-do list for time management has several benefits. A to-do list forces you to focus on the most important tasks. Writing them down makes them more manageable and helps you focus. You can cross things off your list as they are done, which gives you a sense of accomplishment that keeps you motivated. As a result, you will get more done in less time.

To-do lists can be short or long-term. Depending on the nature of your to-do list, you may need both. For instance, long-term goals are difficult to complete in one day. A short-term list may be useful to remember a deadline. For a long-term list, you may need to store reminders for each task separately. You can also write down tasks and due dates.

A to-do list may be long, but you shouldn't make it too long. It's best to start with a small list and work your way up to more difficult tasks. Ideally, you can check off as many tasks as possible every day. And don't worry if you don't complete a task today - it won't matter tomorrow! This method has proven to be effective for many people.

A to-do list helps you stay organized. Having a to-do list keeps your head on your shoulders. Make sure you have it visible and accessible. By separating your tasks into categories, you can see which ones are more important, and which ones need to be done now. This method will keep you focused on the most important tasks first. Then you'll get the rest of your work done.

Chapter 17 - Improving Your Emotional Self-Regulation

A key component of managing your stress is emotion regulation. When our bodies experience high levels of stress, anxiety, or sadness, we must regulate our emotions so we can feel better. But this is easier said than done. If you suffer from emotional dysregulation, you may not be able to control your emotions.

Primary emotions

The primary emotions we feel are often the most immediate. They arise immediately when an event occurs. They are not based on thought, and may even be triggered by the presence of an external stimulus. Some examples include winning the lottery or the loss of a loved one. It's best to avoid situations where your emotions are strong and are accompanied by cognitive processing. But there are also many situations that call for a more nuanced approach.

Despite their similarity, these emotions can be very different. The same primary emotion can be either a feeling of joy or anxiety, or it can be the result of an intensely negative experience. An example of a negative primary emotion is guilt. This emotion can be experienced by a person in situations where they feel worthless or helpless. While all primary emotions can be helpful in some circumstances, they are not universally helpful in others.

The good news is that there are several ways to recognize your emotions and make them more manageable. One way is to make a list of your primary emotions. This will help you identify which emotions you're feeling in a certain situation, and guide you toward solutions. The second technique is to identify what's causing the feelings, and then try to transform them into something that is less upsetting. Regardless of the method you choose, the key to successfully managing emotions is to be aware of them.

There is a growing body of evidence that people experience multiple emotions. The two-factor theory, which includes cognition, argues that emotions are created in the social and cognitive domains and are not inherited in a biological manner. This model explains the differences between cultures, and argues that emotions are not triggered but are instead socially constructed. This approach is known as the theory of constructed emotion. So what are the main factors that influence the regulation of our emotions?

Self-expression

While it may seem difficult to let your emotions be known, you can learn to express yourself better. You don't have to be an acclaimed poet, a star athlete, or a singer to learn how to express yourself. The key to self-expression is identifying uncomfortable feelings and expressing them with tact. It's important to avoid denying your feelings or trying to hide them from others, which can lead to negative consequences.

Psychotherapy and bodywork training can help you discover new ways to express yourself in new situations. Activities such as dance and martial arts can help you release feelings and build resilience. Yoga can reduce stress and give you a new way to express yourself. And learning a new sport can help you explore your physical and mental strengths. Whatever the case, self-expression is key to your overall health and happiness. Self-expression exercises can be a lifesaver.

Impaired ability to regulate emotions

The term "emotional dysregulation" describes the condition of being unable to control one's emotions, particularly anger, anxiety, and depression. Impaired ability to control your emotions can lead to regrettable behaviors and relationships, which are detrimental to your health and your work performance. Many psychological disorders result from impaired ability to regulate emotions. Cognitive behavioral therapy has increasingly adopted an interactive-ontogenetic model of these disorders. However, the exact cause of emotional dysregulation is unknown, and there are currently no definitive studies.

This study showed that manipulation of ER goals reduced amygdala activity and increased activity in brain regions associated with emotion regulation, including the ventrolateral prefrontal cortex and the dorsolateral prefrontal cortex. However, there was no significant difference in activity in the control group, indicating that the role of implicit and explicit ERs is not dissociated. The findings confirm the ER hypothesis and demonstrate that it is important to consider how ER manipulations may be affected in patients with depression.

Chapter 18 - How to Read a History and Physical Examination (H&P)

An H&P is a written report of a patient's health condition. A H&P can vary in length, depending on the clinical situation and complexity of the case. The optimal length of an H&P allows the physician to clearly communicate the facts and emphasize the reliability of the information provided. The first part of the report is the chief complaint, which describes the patient's presenting symptoms. It may be written in the patient's words, or in the appropriate medical terminology.

Structure

The structure of a patient history and physical examination (H&P) will depend on the specific disease or illness being presented and the author's background and experience. While the history and physical examination may not include details like coronary risk factors, the writer will become more focused with experience. Seeking feedback and reading sample write-ups will speed up the process. The core aspects of an H&P are discussed below. In addition, the sample write-ups are intended as reference standards.

Ideally, the H&P should be chronologically organized, telling the story of why the patient is seeking medical attention. The health history section should mention all relevant medical conditions, including any that may be chronic, and can be found in the patient's opening line or past medical history. The history section should also contain any pertinent laboratory results.

Reading style

The reading style of H&P is influenced by several factors, including the type of medical record and the complexity of the case. The length of an H&P can vary widely, but it should be adequate to convey the facts of the patient's condition. The primary goal of the write-up is to emphasize reliability and clarity of communication. The chief complaint is the main feature of the report and should be written in the patient's own words, or in appropriate medical terminology.

How to Read History and Physicals

When reviewing a history and physical, the nurse should review the examination in light of recent information regarding the diagnosis. For example, a chest X-ray revealing a large pleural effusion should prompt the nurse to percuss the patient's chest to hear dullness. Likewise, an echocardiogram may reveal aortic stenosis. This information can be helpful in refining technique and preparing for potential abnormal findings.

The physical examination is an essential part of interpreting a history. The results of the physical examination will confirm or disprove suspicions in the history and raise new questions. Physical examination techniques can range from simple observation to the use of a stethoscope.

A complete physical examination covers the entire body, from head to toe. It will take about 30 minutes to complete. During the exam, the examiner will check vital signs and evaluate the body using various methods. A nurse or physician may perform this physical exam according to their training and education. These methods may include examining the eyes, ears, nose, throat, skin color, and lesions. A physical examination may also involve palpation, checking organ sizes, and monitoring responses.

The patient's medical history should be discussed during the physical examination. The nurse should be concerned about the patient's comfort and make sure the patient feels comfortable during the exam. Prior to the physical exam, the healthcare professional will usually take the patient's history. The medical history is an important part of a physical because it records current symptoms and any previous problems.

Chapter 19 - Pathophysiology - Importance in Home Health

The three Ps of nursing education - Pathophysiology, Pharmacology, and Physical Assessment - are all incredibly important aspects of nursing. This section explains how each P affects students' ability to perform physical examinations. By providing a hands-on approach, the nurse integrates the three Ps into a holistic approach that helps them develop a deeper understanding of their profession.

The Importance of Pathophysiology for Nurses

Understanding pathophysiology is essential for nursing. You better understand abnormal changes in the body and what treatments can be used to correct them. Knowing the pathophysiology of a disease will help you better communicate with doctors and patients, helping you to provide the best care possible for every patient.

Knowing the pathophysiology of a disease or disorder helps nurses identify their primary responsibilities. For example, nurses must understand how to recognize heart failure and what they can do to prevent the patient from suffering from worse outcomes. Pathophysiology is an important part of nursing and every nurse should master this subject.

As another example, you may need to monitor a patient with Bell's palsy, a sudden weakness of facial muscles that prevents the patient from drinking through a straw. Understanding pathophysiology also helps you set more effective nursing priorities and provide better care. Nursing schools emphasize critical thinking skills, which is important for a nurse's role in a medical setting.

Experienced nurses are likely to have a vast amount of experience in dealing with specific patient populations. This knowledge enables them to create comparisons and distinctions. It creates a "matrix" of background expectations and detective work for the patient. As a result, the clinician's focus shifts as predictable changes in a patient's condition occur. The clinician will be prepared for a variety of situations.

Here is list of just some disease topics the home health nurse should review:

CARDIAC:

- Atherosclerosis
- Coronary Artery Disease (CAD)
- Endocarditis
- Heart Failure (CHF)
- Hypertension (HTN)
- Peripheral Arterial Disorder (PAD)
- Peripheral Venous Disorder (PVD)
- Deep Venous Thrombosis (DVT)
- Arrhythmias
- Atrial fibrillation

DERMATOLOGY:

- Cellulitis
- Melanoma
- Dermatitis
- Eczema

- Psoriasis

- Candidiasis

- Stevens-Johnson Syndrome (SJS)

- Diabetic foot

- Pressure Ulcers/Pressure Injuries (and staging)

- Lice

- Scabies

EARS, EYES, NOSE, THROAT (EENT):

- Otorrhea

- Tinnitus

- Hearing loss

- Dizziness and vertigo

- Otitis

- Glaucoma

- Retinopathy (i.e. diabetic retinopathy)

- Cataracts

- Epistaxis

- Nystagmus

- Laryngitis

- Nasal infections

- Rhinitis

- Sinusitis

• ENDOCRINE AND METABOLIC:

- Acid-Base Disorders
- Cushing Syndrome
- Addison Disease
- Pheochromocytoma
- Aldosteronism
- Diabetes Mellitus (type I and type II)
- Diabetic Ketoacidosis (DKA)
- Hyperglycemia and hypoglycemia
- Electrolyte disorders (hypo/hypernatremia, hypo/hyperkalemia, hypo/hypercalcemia, etc.)
- Volume overload
- Dyslipidemia
- Hyperlipidemia (HLD)
- Hypothyroidism

• GASTROINTESTINAL:

- Hemorrhoids
- Gastroesophageal reflux disease (GERD)
- Diverticulitis
- Dysphagia
- Gastritis
- Peptic ulcer
- Gastroenteritis

- GI bleed
- Inflammatory bowel disease (IBD)
- Irritable bowel syndrome (IBS)
- Celiac disease
- Pancreatitis
- Bowel incontinence
- Obesity

GENITOURINARY:

- Acute kidney injury (AKI)
- Benign Prostatic Hyperplasia (BPH)
- Chronic Kidney Disease (CKD)
- Diabetic nephropathy
- Urinary calculi
- Urinary tract infection (UTI)
- Pyelonephritis
- Neurogenic bladder
- Urinary retention
- Urinary incontinence

COMMON IN GERIATRICS:

- Elder abuse
- Falls in older people
- Gait disorders
- Polypharmacy

- Isolation
- Frailty
- Self-neglect
- End-of-life care

HEMATOLOGY AND ONCOLOGY:

- Cancers
- Anemias
- Coagulation disorders
- Eosinophilia
- Leukemia
- Lymphomas
- Splenomegaly
- Thrombocytopenia

HEPATIC AND BILIARY:

- Liver injury
- Cirrhosis
- Cholecystitis
- Cholelithiasis
- Hepatitis
- Hepatic cysts

MUSCULOSKELETAL:

- Sjögren Syndrome

- Systemic Lupus Erythematosus (SLE)
- Multiple Sclerosis (MS)
- Bursitis
- Fibromyalgia
- Tendonitis
- Gout
- Plantar fasciitis
- Carpal tunnel syndrome
- Osteoarthritis
- Osteomyelitis
- Rheumatoid arthritis
- Sciatica
- Lumbar spinal stenosis
- Osteoporosis
- Total hip replacement (total hip arthroplasty)
- Total knee replacements (total knee arthroplasty or TKA)

NEUROLOGIC:

- Encephalitis
- Delirium
- Dementia
- Alzheimer's
- Multiple sclerosis
- Aphasia

- Migraine

- Meningitis

- Parkinson disease

- Trigeminal neuralgia

- Acute pain

- Chronic pain

- Neuropathic pain

- Guillain-Barré Syndrome (GBS)

- Amyotrophic Lateral Sclerosis (ALS)

- Myasthenia Gravis

- Seizures

- Insomnia

- Narcolepsy

- Acute cerebrovascular accident (stroke or CVA)

- Ischemic stroke

- Transient ischemic attack (TIA)

- Subarachnoid hemorrhage

PSYCHIATRIC:

- Anxiety (acute)

- Generalized anxiety disorder (GAD)

- Post-traumatic stress disorder (PTSD)

- Eating disorders (Anorexia and bulimia)

- Bipolar disorders

- Depression

- Major depressive disorder

- Obsessive compulsive disorder (OCD)

- Schizophrenia

PULMONARY:

- Acute bronchitis

- Asthma

- Bronchiectasis and Atelectasis

- Chronic Obstructive Pulmonary Disease (COPD)

- Pneumonia

- Tuberculosis (TB)

- Pulmonary Embolism (PE)

- Pulmonary hypertension

- Obstructive Sleep Apnea (OSA)

- COVID-19

This list is not exhaustive, and nurses should keep on the lookout to building on top of their current knowledge of pathophysiology. It is best to review the diseases system by system. Tip: Use the free resource MerckManuals.com to as a good database for review of pathophysiology topics.

Understanding disease and its pathophysiology is essential for nurses. The knowledge of the causes of disease, its symptoms, and treatment methods will help them provide effective care for patients. Nursing practitioners benefit from critical thinking skills, which help them implement timely preventive measures. The use of critical thinking skills is essential in pathophysiology.

Communication skills are key for a nursing career. However, it is important to be sensitive to cultural differences. Developing empathy and compassion are key to being a good nurse.

Chapter 20 - Pharmacology - Medications to Review

A sound understanding of pharmacology is essential for nurses. This will ensure minimal errors. Nurses are expected to administer the correct medications to the right patients or teach the patient or their caregivers proper administration techniques. Proper knowledge of pharmacology will enable them to correctly assess patients. This knowledge greatly contributes to the minimal errors that nurses commit

Drug-drug interactions

Despite their importance, drug-drug interactions are often overlooked by nurses. According to a survey, 40% of nurses reported observing a drug interaction in their clinical practice in the past year. Although many nurses were aware of potential drug interactions, few explored them in-depth. Many nurses use alternative resources to identify possible drug-drug interactions, such as handbooks and colleagues. In addition, few nurses have access to clinical pharmacists or computer programs to identify potential drug-drug interactions.

The number of drugs on the market makes drug therapy complex, and the possibility of drug-drug interactions increases every day. Nurses must be aware of these interactions, as they can influence the patient's response to a given drug. Because of this, good communication among health care team members is critical. Patients with chronic conditions and those taking multiple medications are at greatest risk for drug interactions. Older adults are particularly susceptible to drug-drug interactions. About 75% of older adults take at least two prescription medications, in addition to a variety of OTC drugs.

Although it is crucial to be aware of drug-drug interactions, a yellow card is the easiest and most obvious way to report these.

Most prescribers use the yellow card. However, the Committee on Safety of Medicines received no reports of a drug-drug interaction with fluoxetine, chlorpromazine, risperidone, or lisinopril. Clearly, there is a need for increased public awareness of drug-drug interactions and to encourage trusts to incorporate reporting into their drug policies.

There are several ways to mitigate these risks. For example, prescribing guidelines should be followed to avoid negative drug interactions. The researchers recommend titrating drug doses and switching to an alternative drug whose metabolism pathway is different. In addition, nurses should monitor the interactions of their patients' current medication regimen. Hopefully, these guidelines will help them make informed decisions when it comes to addressing these issues. They may even help nurses identify a new medication that is not currently available.

One of the most important aspects of identifying and treating drug-drug interactions is to ensure adequate surveillance. This means that nurses have the ability to avoid potentially dangerous drug combinations. Furthermore, adequate surveillance systems will allow them to prevent clinical problems. Additionally, prescribing indicators should focus on identifying potential DDIs and alternative treatment options. That way, nurses will have the best knowledge to determine when a drug-drug interaction may occur.

Another important way to prevent negative drug interactions is to keep track of the dosages and types of drugs in the patient's medication. Over-the-counter and prescription drugs often have warning labels. However, these warnings do not contain all warnings and should not be relied upon as a substitute for careful consultation with a physician. Moreover, they should always discuss the drug with their patients before prescribing any medication.

Grouping drugs into classes

In nursing, you must know how to classify drugs. Drugs are classified based on their effect on specific body systems and their potential for misuse. This is known as pharmacology. Pharmacology also classes drugs based on their schedules. The control of drug use in the 1960s led to the creation of five schedules for drugs. These schedules were intended to make prescribing and monitoring medications easier.

To better understand drug effects, you must understand the dose of a given drug. As a nurse, you must pay close attention to the anticipated effect as well as to the response of the patient. You must also be aware of the overall dose-response relationship and how to adjust the dose to get the best response. Each drug has a peak, duration, and onset of action. These characteristics are affected by the route of administration, GI tract capacity, and the patency of the circulatory system. A drug's peak concentration is usually where it produces the greatest therapeutic effect.

To increase the level of engagement in pharmacology classes, faculty can incorporate social media into the teaching process. Students can interact with faculty members through videos, web-based quizzes, or blogs. These strategies promote student engagement while increasing retention. Moreover, they also help improve student understanding of the material. Ultimately, social media integration is vital for nursing students' success in pharmacology.

Despite the fact that pharmacology courses are important for nursing students, many universities and colleges are striving to improve the quality of teaching in the field. Students are increasingly demanding and expect support during their studies. Thus, educators have devised a variety of learning strategies to help nursing students understand the complexities of the subject. A pharmacology course can make or break a nursing student's career, so it is essential to provide adequate pharmacology instruction in order to meet this goal.

Students who take pharmacology courses are expected to learn complicated concepts through interactive online learning and face-to-face classroom interaction. These strategies can help students engage with the course content and help them master difficult pharmacological concepts. However, they can also enhance their performance in online or classroom assessments. So, if you're a nurse who teaches online, consider using innovative teaching methods to increase the level of student engagement in your pharmacology course.

In addition to combining traditional and digital learning methods, game-based learning has proven to be highly effective. Kahoot allows instructors to create multiple-choice questions that students can answer in small groups. These tests provide immediate feedback and create friendly competition among students. In addition to gamified learning methods, Kahoot is an excellent tool for nursing students to enhance their knowledge of pharmacology.

Medications to Review

Below is a list of just some of classification of medications to review:

- Adrenergics

- Adrenocortical steroids

- Analgesics

- Antacids/adsorbents/antiflatulents

- Anti-anginal

- Anti-arthritic/anti-gout

- Anti-arrythmics

- Antibiotics
- Anticholinergics
- Anticoagulants
- Anticonvulsants
- Antidepressants
- Anti-diabetic orals
- Anti-diabetic insulins
- Antihistamines
- Antilipidemics
- Antihypertensives
- Antiparkinson
- Antiplatelets
- Antipyretics
- Cardiac gylcosides
- Cholinergics
- Diuretics
- Electrolyte replenishers
- Laxatives
- Muscle relaxants
- Opthalmics
- Sedatives/anti-anxiety
- Spasmolytics/bronchodilators
- GI tract drugs

- Major tranquilizers
- Vasodilators
- Anticonvulsants
- Anti-diarrheal
- Anti-emetic
- Antifungal
- Antipsychotic
- Antiviral
- Arthritis meds
- BPH meds
- Cough meds
- Decongestants
- Expectorants/antitussives
- GERD meds
- Memory enhancers
- Neurogenic bladder meds
- Neuropathic meds
- Restless leg syndrome mds
- Skin barriers
- Thyroid meds
- Topical antifungals
- Topical antibacterials
- Topical antiparasitics

- Topical antiviral

- Topical corticosteroids

And of course review vitamins and minerals and nutritional supplements. It is also important to be familiar with complementary and alternative therapies. While not exhaustive, this list provides a brief overview of the common classification of medications you will see in home health. Tip: See MedScape.com for a further detailed database of medications for you to review.

Understanding pharmacodynamics

Pharmacology is an important subject for nurses, as it determines how well drugs work in the body. Pharmacodynamics is the study of the biochemical changes that occur in the body as a result of drug concentration. It also involves the post-receptor effects of drugs. In order for nurses to be effective in their practice, they must understand the processes of drug absorption and metabolism. The following article will explain these processes in more detail.

The term "pharmacodynamics" describes the actions of a drug in the body. Specifically, it relates to how long a drug takes to work. The duration and extent of a drug's effect is measured in terms of Emax. This is the maximum effect of the drug on a parameter, such as platelet inhibition in an ex-vivo test or the greatest lowering of blood pressure.

When it comes to administering medications, the role of a nurse is to monitor the condition of patients, communicate with physicians, and give them medications. To do this successfully, nurses must understand pharmacodynamics, pharmacokinetics, and the physiological interactions of drugs. Fortunately, a Bradley online Doctor of Nursing Practice - Family Nurse Practitioner program can equip you with the knowledge and skills necessary to successfully handle pharmacology in the patient.

The material on Understanding Pharmacodynamics for Nurses is a comprehensive study that will help nurses and other healthcare professionals learn how to safely administer drugs. Upon completion, the course credits six contact hours for the online independent study activity. It provides essential knowledge of drug pharmacokinetics and pharmacodynamics and their applications. Using pharmacological knowledge will be an invaluable tool to help nurses manage patients in the long run.

Understanding the process of drug absorption and dissolution helps nursing professionals make better decisions when prescribing medications. The process of monitoring drug levels includes peak and trough levels. Peak levels are the highest concentrations, while trough levels are the lowest. Keeping track of these drug levels is important to prevent overdose and underdose. High peak levels can cause toxicity and low trough levels can mitigate an intended effect.

Pharmacokinetics outlines the actions of drugs in the body. Excessive medication can cause serious adverse effects. Toxic medications can cause organ, system, or even fatal effects. When the body is unable to eliminate or metabolize a drug, it builds up in the blood, and is thus considered toxic. These side effects are often unexpected and can result in dangerous interactions or even fatal outcomes. Understanding pharmacodynamics for nurses helps nurses understand how drugs work and how to avoid them.

Chapter 21 - Physical Assessment - Importance for Nurses

The importance of a thorough physical assessment for nurses cannot be overstated. By performing a complete physical examination, nurses establish the baseline of a patient's medical diagnosis and presenting symptoms. Physical assessment also ensures the safety and security of a patient. The second-leading cause of sentinel events is an incorrect assessment of the patient's condition. Performing complete physical assessments will allow nurses to pick up subtle signs of changes in the patient's condition and may prevent incidents such as failure to rescue, falls, infection, or failure to treat.

Examining the entire body

Nursing care includes various methods of assessment. One of these methods is the physical examination. Nurses evaluate a patient's condition by performing a physical examination. They may use an ultrasound to determine a patient's size, contour, and symmetry. An ultrasound can also help identify organ size and shape. Nurses can also perform auscultation using an unaided ear or with the assistance of mechanical devices.

Nurses should develop a positive relationship with patients and be sensitive to the cultural needs of patients. By developing trust, patients are more likely do reveal information that they would otherwise not disclose to someone they will close themselves off to. To achieve this, they must provide a private, quiet environment for the patient to complete their history and physical examination. A classic physical examination begins with the head and proceeds through the body.

A nurse must know the difference between normal and abnormal findings. Abnormalities can be difficult to detect but can indicate problems with respiratory or musculoskeletal systems. In addition to visual observations, nurses also use the sense of touch to make accurate diagnoses. By palpating different parts of the body, a nurse can evaluate size and mobility. They can also identify tenderness. These methods are essential in assessing patient comfort and safety.

Performing a physical examination consists of several procedures. Nurses use four basic methods when performing a physical examination. The first method of examination involves sight and smell. Nurses examine various body parts for normal color, shape, and consistency. Once they determine that the patient is normal, they can perform a comprehensive physical examination. Once they know which areas of the body are healthy, they can determine what other procedures may need to be performed.

Using sight, sound, and smell

In the realm of physical assessment, nurses will learn to evaluate the patient through their senses. Physical assessment techniques include inspection, palpation, and auscultation. They will learn to perform a head-to-toe physical examination, beginning with an overall inspection to assess the patient's condition and then focusing on the eyes, ears, and nose to gather information. In this way, nurses will be prepared for a variety of physical examination situations that could arise, including a patient's medical history.

During a physical assessment, nurses should be able to determine the type of nursing care the patient needs. They should also ensure the safety of the client and contribute to the medical field by assessing the medical fitness of the client. This type of assessment involves a systematic visual examination that involves deliberate purposeful observation. It includes the ability to determine symmetry, size, and position. Using the sense of smell and hearing is also essential when performing this type of examination.

The physical assessment is not a complete work-up; nurses should focus on any extreme abnormalities, such as bleeding or damage to vital organs. Otherwise, the provider may order further diagnostics. The SBAR model bridges the gap between narrative and the SBAR approach. When using the SBAR approach, nurses can evaluate the patient's physical condition and communicate with the healthcare team. They can also use the assessment findings to make recommendations for care.

Nurses can practice by watching example videos of assessments. For example, watch a video of a nurse performing a detailed head-to-toe assessment. The video will show you how to perform the assessment, including the steps involved, and the nurse explains the process. You can even ask the patient questions before touching them.

Assessing internal organs

The primary survey includes a nurse's observation of the patient's breathing, skin color, pulse, capillary refill time, and gas exchange. She also collects data on the client's breathing and gas exchange to determine how well he or she is able to communicate. Additionally, she examines the patient's internal organs. After the primary survey, she then conducts a secondary survey to determine the patient's condition.

One of the most basic ways to determine the condition of an internal organ is to tap it against the patient's body. Using the non-dominant hand's middle finger, percussion can reveal the organ's shape and size. It can also reveal whether it is fluid-filled or air-filled. If the organ is painful, it is best to apply deep pressure to determine if it's bleeding or inflamed.

When palpating the abdomen, the nurse should listen to the heartbeat, and assess for any differences between the heart's sound and the patient's. Patients over the age of 12 should be positioned in the supine position, which is the most comfortable position for the patient. Other positions to evaluate the internal organs include the prone position, which allows for hip joint extension and skin and buttock flexion. The dorsal and lateral recumbent positions are recommended for the assessment of painful disorders or those involving the muscles.

During the primary assessment, the nurse uses a stethoscope on the patient's bare skin to listen to the patient's heartbeat, lungs, and abdominal functions. An additional examination involves the use of specific devices, including the tongue depressor. These tools help the nurse gather important information that can inform the patient's health care plan. The final step is the documentation of the findings.

Documenting findings in the EMR

While physical assessments are an important part of the nursing process, they're not always documented properly. Using the "next best" option instead of documenting the findings in the EHR can lead to miscommunication and clinical errors. Adding notes is a better way to capture vital information and avoid note bloat. This article explores some of the challenges and best practices for documentation. Here are three tips to help improve physical assessment documentation.

When you're doing a physical assessment, you'll want to document both subjective and objective data. Objective data can be collected from several sources, including patient reports. Subjective data should be documented in quotation marks. It's best to start with a patient's report when documenting subjective data. The key to collecting valuable subjective data is developing rapport. In addition to using quotation marks to show your findings, you'll want to make sure you include any measurements or observations you took.

The timer data in the EHR is useful for tracking timers. You can use them to measure when you start and end documentation. The timer data was validated by video recording of sample nurses completing the forms. You can also compare the system timers with video recording timers to make sure the system is accurate. By using an EMR, you'll have a clear documentation trail that can be used to defend yourself in a legal case.

Not recording bowel sounds can also lead to medical errors. For example, a harried nurse may miss a bowel sound during abdominal auscultation. Consequently, the patient may develop abdominal pain and vomiting. If this is the case, the nurse could be held legally responsible for the delayed treatment. Documentation is an essential nursing responsibility. It helps you plan care, communicate with other providers, and prove compliance with regulations. Ultimately, an improperly documented patient assessment can result in a professional liability lawsuit or even action against a nurse's license.

Importance of conversation with the patient

A nurse's job requires a great deal of communication skills. This includes the ability to listen carefully to a patient's concerns and to ask questions that will help her explore those concerns. To be successful, she must speak clearly, avoid using jargon, and use familiar terms whenever possible. In addition, she must acknowledge each patient's statement, even if it is not in agreement with it. This can be as simple as a question, such as "Does that sound right?".

During the physical assessment, the nurse should start by getting to know the patient. This can be done by looking at their previous records and asking questions about their concerns. She should always show compassion and listen without judgment. She should ask about their concerns and beliefs. She should also ask about their goals in life and what motivates them. In addition, she should ask about any misconceptions or fears that the patient may have.

While open-ended questioning is beneficial in gathering general information, closed-ended questioning can be helpful in urgent situations. However, nurses should always be sure not to draw too many conclusions from short answers. The nurse should also make sure to acknowledge the patient's response and encourage discussion with phrases. A great way to do this is by using appropriate intonations and phrases. They should also use body language to build connections with the patient and improve their overall experience of their visits.

When conducting a physical examination, the nurse should use several techniques to facilitate the conversation with the patient. One of the most important techniques is to ask the patient about their concerns. It is important for a nurse to understand how medical terminology affects their patients, as many patients feel embarrassed to ask for clarification. Inappropriately-phrased questions can lead to inaccurate data collection. Also, a patient who feels judged and attacked may respond in an angry or defensive manner and give incorrect information.

If patients end up not liking you, they will not share the information you need to do your job well and it could affect your job performance as a result. This is why building trust and rapport with the patient is key to effectively gathering data.

Chapter 22 - Driving Safety For Home Health Nurses

The need for in-home care is increasing, thanks to a booming aging population and fear of contagion. Many people also want to age in place, and that means home health nurses are in high demand. However, home visiting nurses pose a significant risk to themselves by entering patients' homes, so they must be particularly vigilant about hand and shoe hygiene, and drive carefully. There are many ways that a nurse can ensure driving safety for home health nurses.

Workplace violence

Home health nurses may be exposed to various types of workplace violence. Workplace violence is an issue that can overwhelm their coping abilities. A prolonged period of stress can adversely affect health. The results of several studies have shown that workplace violence may lead to poorer mental and physical health outcomes. In addition, it may affect interpersonal interactions between the home care worker and consumer-employer. Ultimately, these conditions may impact the quality of care.

Musculoskeletal injuries

Drivers who are home health nurses are especially at risk for musculoskeletal disorders. The risk for musculoskeletal injuries is particularly high among new drivers who are not used to driving in heavy traffic. This problem is particularly troubling in the context of a nursing shortage, where an aging workforce is depleting the nursing workforce and retention rates are falling.

Despite this, it is still essential to follow the laws regarding the safe driving practices of home health nurses. The law requires home health nurses to follow strict traffic safety regulations.

Moreover, home health nurses should also wear seat belts that offer a firm support. Musculoskeletal injuries while driving for home health nurses may result in a car accident. Therefore, home health nurses should avoid driving while undergoing anything that may distract them from the road.

The American Nurses Association's position statement on musculoskeletal disorders is a call to action to prevent these conditions. In addition to calling for safe driving practices, the statement also calls for a health care industry-wide effort to prevent work-related musculoskeletal injuries. Nursing positions are prone to these musculoskeletal disorders. Hence, the ANA urges nurses to make sure they are properly trained.

Neighborhood assessment

Nurses who deliver home health care services should use an effective risk assessment tool when making patient visits. The tool uses a scoring system to determine crime and hazard areas. It is a useful tool to monitor crime rates and number of police calls. Another tool for risk assessment is a windshield survey. Staff should be able to recognize the difference between typical activity and something out of the ordinary. A team of security professionals from VNSNY will contact the precinct to confirm that the activity is unusual.

Emergency preparedness

The best way to ensure your business is prepared for any foreseeable event is to have a disaster plan. Developing this plan can help you ensure you can provide the best possible care to the victims of disasters. It also helps to develop a hazard vulnerability analysis and comprehensive emergency planning to ensure that everything is handled smoothly. By implementing these steps, you can ensure that your home health care business is prepared for any unforeseen event.

Disasters are becoming a tough teacher. Each one of them allows us to learn from previous disasters and integrate them into our practice. For example, during the devastating fires in Fort McMurray, nurses were called to help burn victims and high-risk patients. These events have resulted in a review of the disaster response process. This review will include the steps home health nurses can take to ensure patient safety during an emergency.

To comply with emergency preparedness requirements, home health nurses must develop a plan for their clients. This plan will include emergency supplies and a plan for dealing with disasters. To ensure you're prepared, you can access templates and guidelines from the Centers for Medicare & Medicaid Services. You can also use the guidelines from Wisconsin Department of Health Services to develop an emergency preparedness plan. And don't forget to follow all of the safety recommendations in the plan!

SECTION 3 – During the Visit

Being Present with the Patient

Chapter 23 - Home Safety For Patients and Nurses

Managing patient safety in the home is a vital part of providing quality care at home. There are many different aspects to consider, from fall risks to medication safety. In addition to reducing patient safety risks, we discuss emergency preparedness and neighborhood safety. These tips will help you plan for and manage your patient's needs when providing care at home.

Neighborhood Safety

Nurses who work in community settings should assess risks and prepare accordingly. Asking questions about the client's residence, the safety of the surrounding neighborhood and any previous incidents of violence are vital parts of preparing for community work. Once you know what the risks are, you can explore ways to mitigate them.

Always protect yourself while you treat patients. For example, in Chicago, homicides tend to concentrate in low-income neighborhoods. A nurse may have a visit to the neighborhood to care for a sick elderly patient. While she is there, mobs gathered and started shooting. When she is there, the best approach to find safety first and then contact the police, terminate the visit, and notify your home health agency.

Mobility and Fall Risk at Home

While fall prevention is an important priority for health care professionals, there are many other concerns for patients, especially those on bed rest. Aside from increasing the risk of injury, falls can cause additional complications and prolong the recovery process. To effectively prevent falls, nurses must assess each patient's fall risk and implement interventions. These measures may include providing individualized instruction, designing safer environments, and implementing frequent reassessments.

The environment surrounding the patient should be assessed for potential fall hazards. Throw rugs and clutter may cause tripping hazards, as can uneven or broken stairs. Other hazards include an unfamiliar environment or floor coverings. Falls can occur even if there are no obstructions on the floor. The environment where the patient works may also pose a fall risk. Unprotected landfills and creeks can also be hazards.

For the nurse, integrating an electronic health record with a validated fall risk assessment tool can be an ideal practice environment. An EHR can also gather concurrent data, such as health evaluations, inpatient and outpatient visits, laboratory and diagnostic tests, and a fall risk assessment tool. These tools allow nurses to use their time more efficiently and collaborate effectively with the interprofessional care team. This allows the nurse to make more informed decisions based on a patient's individual risk factors and care goals.

Medication Safety at Home for Patients

In hospitals or at home, medication mistakes are often the result of interruptions. Among these distractions are cell phones, radios, TVs, and other devices. To prevent mistakes, keep medications out of reach from children and pets and store them in original containers. When giving medication to patients, identify yourself and let health care providers know about all of your medications and any allergies you may have. You should also make sure that they are familiar with your list of medications and understand which ones you need to continue taking at home after you leave the hospital. Whenever possible, ask for generic brand versions of medications and verify your prescriptions.

The safety of medication cannot be taken for granted. Despite this, a patient's knowledge about his or her medication may be underestimated. Patients may try household tricks to improve adherence. Nurses and pharmacists must be aware of potential problems and share information with patients and caregivers to improve care. When providing home healthcare to elderly patients, it is essential to ensure the patient's medication safety and the safety of the caregiver.

Emergency Preparedness at Home

Nurses and patients alike should be aware of disaster preparedness plans. The first step to respond to an incident is to recognize the emergency and begin preparedness efforts. External responses may include search and rescue operations, firefighting, or building shelters for the displaced. In order to protect their patients and themselves, nurses should have a clear understanding of the disaster plan and events surrounding the event. In the case of the Fort McMurray, Alberta, fire, nurses needed to prepare for large-scale care for burn victims and many others.

The federal government has set specific guidelines for health care facilities to follow during an emergency. These guidelines require nursing homes and 16 other types of facilities to be prepared to provide care to patients in the event of a disaster. Emergency preparedness plans should include procedures and guidelines for communicating with patients and family members during an emergency. The American Health Care Association recommends that nursing facilities make their plans available to its members and staff.

Fire Hazard at Home

One of the most common causes of injury and death in the United States is high-rise building fires. Recent HR building fires serve as high-profile reminders of this public health threat.

Fire safety is a critical issue that community/public health nurses should discuss.

As a rule, a hospitals and even at home should check its equipment and outlets regularly. The batteries should be changed if the smoke detector beeps frequently. It is also vital to clear all obstructions from sprinkler heads to prevent water from spraying on a fire. Electrical cords should be properly plugged into outlets and not overloaded. Also, electrical cords should not be too frayed or damaged.

Bathroom Safety at Home

The first step to improving bathroom safety at home is to make it easy for your loved one to use the bathroom. Having toiletries within reach and seating around the sink are important safety measures. A seat can help prevent falls, but may not be possible in a small bathroom. A motion-activated night light can provide adequate illumination. A secure and clean bathroom can help prevent slips and falls, so keep it clean.

In addition to grab bars, consider installing a weighted shower curtain in the bathroom. It will keep water from splashing out of the shower and onto the bathroom floor. You can also ask your health care provider for a referral to an occupational therapist. They can visit your home to inspect the bathroom and make recommendations for making it safer. The bathroom is the second most dangerous place in the house, so make sure you have a grab bar in every bathroom.

You can also assess the bathroom's safety. A bathroom that is small and has a high toilet seat can improve safety. Even a modest bathroom with a high toilet seat can be safe, but you'll need tools to install safety bars. Other bathroom safety tips include removing toiletries and installing non-slip mats. Installing a toilet seat lift is a great way to improve safety.

Adding grab bars to a toilet can also help an older person transfer into and out of the shower.

Infection Control at Home

Infection prevention and control (IPC) is a practical, evidence-based approach to preventing harm to health care providers and patients. Infection control practices reduce the risk of transmission of infection, promote good hygiene and reduce the impact of antimicrobial resistance. Nurses need to know the most common barriers to infection control practices in hospitals, outpatient clinics, and the home environment.

A key part of prevention is education. CDC has developed a series of training resources to help front-line staff protect patients and keep healthcare workers safe from infection. It also includes letters to families about the COVID-19 vaccine and information on how to protect patients and staff. CDC infection prevention guidelines include a hand-hygiene program. Infection control training should be integrated into the quality management program of any agency.

Chapter 24 - The Bag Technique for Home Health Nurses

When caring for a patient, hand hygiene is critical to the prevention of infection. You will learn about the benefits and best practices of the bag technique, including how to implement it in a home health setting.

Choosing a nursing bag

While home health nurses carry large amounts of supplies during the day, nurses working in acute care settings may need only a penlight and stethoscope. Other supplies may be available in the facility. In either case, choosing a nursing bag with sufficient compartments is important. The following are some things to look for in a nursing bag:

- Designed with several compartments, a home health nurse's bag should be easy to carry and has separate clean and dirty compartments. It should also be waterproof and sturdy enough to hold all the supplies a nurse needs for a single visit. The interior of a home health nurse's bag should include mesh storage pouches and a lockable HIPAA-compliant folder.

- Large compartments: When choosing a nursing bag, make sure the compartments are large enough to fit the tools a nurse will use in a single visit. A canvas bag with plenty of pockets is ideal for travel and can accommodate a small notebook and several medical instruments. A bag with a large interior will be more convenient when you need to bring a laptop or other electronic devices. - A large size will be comfortable for carrying.

- Fabric: When selecting a nursing bag, consider the fabric. Some nursing bags are made from tough cloth. However, it's important to keep in mind that fabrics cannot be thoroughly disinfected. A nursing bag made of vinyl or leather is a great choice if you need a durable bag. Make sure to research the brand of nursing bags so you can find a nursing bag that suits your needs.

- Comfort and storage: Depending on your needs, the size of your work bag should be an important consideration. If you need a lot of storage, choose a nursing bag with plenty of compartments and easy-to-clean materials. If it doesn't have enough compartments, consider purchasing a travel organizer bag. These will keep your gear organized and easily accessible. Once you've found a nursing bag that meets all your requirements, your home health nurse will thank you for it for years to come.

Cleaning the outside regularly

A nurse should clean the outside of their home healthcare bag at least weekly. This requires using disinfectant wipes or hand washing every month. Depending on the type of bag, some may be hand washable while others require a disinfectant spray. If there are electronic items in the bag, they should be disinfected at least monthly. The staff should use their best judgment when selecting a place to work. The room should be clean, well lit, low traffic, and free from any pets.

Nurses should never leave their bags in the front seat of a vehicle to avoid spreading pathogens. Cleaning the outside regularly of nursing bags will reduce the risk of spreading illness to patients. In addition, if the bags are visible, nurses should disinfect them immediately. A clean nursing bag will make the job easier for them. Cleaning the outside of your bag will keep your supplies and patient belongings safe from contamination.

Never put your bag on the floor while inside the patient's home while performing care. You can kindly ask the patient or their family where you can safely place your bag, either or a chair or table. While placing your bag in your car, you should have a special container just for your bag that keeps it separate from other items in your car.

Cleaning the inside of the bag

The proper method of cleaning the inside of the bag for home health nurses is crucial to prevent the spread of bacteria and other contagious agents. When you're transporting patient equipment and supplies, you must clean your bag after using it. You need to keep your bag as sterile as possible. Your patients' health depends on it! Clean your bag and all of your equipment frequently, and you'll be more likely to provide excellent care.

First, clean the reusable items in your home health nurse's bag after using them. These items should be cleaned after every patient and disinfected before repackaging. Many nurses do this once a week, but some even clean it every month or so. If you notice that your bag is visibly soiled, you should clean it immediately. You can also reuse the bag's contents for another patient.

After each visit, you should wipe the inside of your home health nurse's supply bag. Disinfectant wipes kill bacteria and viruses and can help prevent the spread of germs. You should also allow the disinfectant to sit on the bag for at least 15 minutes. Then, remove the bag from the patient's home health nurse's bag and store it in a clean area of the car.

To clean the inside of the bag, place the flap of the clinician's bag away from the floor of the patient's home. A hanger or doorknob is a convenient place to hang the bag. The bag should remain closed while the clinician is not actively obtaining items. Do not load it too heavily as it may tip over. In addition to this, make sure to clean the outside of the bag frequently. If it's visibly dirty, you can wipe it off with a damp towel.

The healthcare bag should be cleaned weekly or at least once a month. This includes disinfecting it with Sani-Cloth and hand washing it with antibacterial solution. Keeping the bag clean is important for the health of the patient and the health of the home. To keep your bag safe, you must keep it near a clean place. You should avoid using the same place for many visits and use a designated corner in your work area to store the bag.

It is imperative that the nursing bag is properly disinfected and cleaned. The presence of human pathogens in the bag should not be a surprise. It has been proven that 48 percent of nursing bags contain infectious agents. In order to avoid contamination of the nursing bag, make sure you wash your hands thoroughly before starting the cleaning process.

Avoiding putting dirty things in your bag

A nurse's bag serves as a portable hospital supply room, holding all of the supplies needed to care for a patient. Because it is likely to become dirty, nurses must be extra careful when they pack their bag. The inside of the bag should be as clean as possible, and only items that are clean and sanitary should be placed in it. Avoid placing dirty items in your bag, and always ask for permission to use the patient's space before opening it.

After a client's care, you should disinfect any items that might have gotten soiled. You can disinfect these items by using 70 percent isopropyl alcohol or an EPA-registered germicidal wipe. Then, place these items in a clean plastic bag and place them back into your bag. You should not put dirty items into your bag, such as a sharps container. Disinfecting items before you return them to the bag is critical for maintaining a clean and safe working environment.

Using a blood pressure cuff

One way to make the BP-measuring process more convenient for patients is to use a bag with a cuff that is inflatable. Inflatable cuffs can be placed on an upper arm about 2 inches above the elbow. The arrow of the cuff should line up with the brachial artery. The patient should stand upright for a minute before you begin the measurement.

To check the BP-measuring device, inflate the cuff until it reaches a level of 130 mmHg. Turn the bulb counterclockwise until the needle drops by two mmHg per second. If the BP-measuring device registers the first sound, the reading is systolic. If it does not drop within that range, the BP-measuring device is ineffective and inaccurate.

The blood pressure-measuring device must be used as part of the home health nurse's home-care service. It must be used by a trained professional who has received adequate training in blood pressure-measuring devices. This technique is often used in home care situations where a nurse is on call 24/7. However, there are several guidelines that home health nurses should follow to ensure the safety of the equipment.

While the sphygmomanometer is a staple of basic medical visits, it can also be personalized. A thermometer is another necessary tool for home care visits. A thermometer should be sanitized after use. You can also customize the thermometer for each patient. But remember to take the plastic bag off each time. This way, you will avoid contamination.

Using a stethoscope to listen to the heart

Using a stethoscope can be helpful for home health nurses who provide reassurance to patients. The instrument is a stethoscope with earpieces that fit into the ears comfortably. Using too-tight earpieces can reduce the quality of sound. Keep the tubing short to reduce background noise. The chest piece should be placed on the part of the body being auscultated.

Depending on the patient's age, the stethoscope may feature a diaphragm or bell.

A nurse's job is to monitor vital body sounds and alert a doctor to changes. A nurse's job may involve monitoring blood pressure and heartbeat to detect abnormalities or illnesses. A nurse is not trained to diagnose diseases or prescribe treatment, but she must listen to vital signs of health. The stethoscope provides home health nurses with a valuable tool to help patients stay healthy.

Auscultation is an excellent way to detect certain diseases. However, it should only be performed by trained medical professionals. Because it is complex and requires special training, an untrained ear cannot differentiate between healthy and unhealthy sounds. A trained ear can distinguish between healthy and abnormal sounds, but an amateur stethoscope is ineffective in this situation. When using a stethoscope to listen to the heart for home health nurses, you should follow the advice of a qualified medical professional.

Using a stethoscope is an excellent way to hear the heart sounds. A stethoscope should be held between your pointing finger and your middle finger. When using a stethoscope, be sure to select a high-quality stethoscope to prevent any damage to the device. Additionally, make sure that the tubing is free of leaks.

Using hand sanitizer

Using hand sanitizer is an important part of the "Bag Technique," which helps prevent the spread of microorganisms from person to person. Although nurses are responsible for washing their hands multiple times per day, the technique must be applied properly to avoid spreading germs. A nurse should also use lotion to keep skin moist and hydrated. Nurses should also carry a notebook with them for taking notes from doctors and observing patients. In addition to a notebook, a nurse may also carry her drug handbook and intravenous medications, a pair of scissors, penlight, a 4 in 1 pen, a towel, a tape measure, and a homemade cheat sheet for patients.

A good bag technique for a home health nurse should include the following information: the purpose of the visit, the type of therapy, and any necessary items. In addition to the bag's contents, home health nurses should also include information about the visit, including the type of hand sanitizer used, any equipment used, and hand hygiene. Sanitizing the hands of home health nurses is an important part of infection management, so it is advisable to follow infection management guidelines and discuss the practice with an infectious disease expert.

Home health nurses should also remember that they should wash their hands before and after touching a patient. A nursing bag should be clean and free from signs of wear and tear. If it is in poor condition, consider purchasing a new bag. Using hand sanitizer as a bag technique can help prevent bag malfunctions, such as when the nursing bag breaks apart during a visit.

Disinfecting items before returning to the bag

After caring for a patient, a nurse should always disinfect supplies in their nursing bag before returning them. To disinfect items, they should use 70 percent isopropyl alcohol or an Environmental Protection Agency-registered germicidal wipe. Once disinfected, they should dry on a barrier and place them back in their bag. Disinfecting items before returning them to the bag for home health nurses should be done at least monthly, but preferably daily.

After returning to a patient's home, the home health nurse should make sure to dispose of items properly. Disinfecting reusable items before returning them to a bag is especially important when they have come into contact with infected patients with antibiotic-resistant infections. They should also double bag reusable items to prevent a cross-contamination problem. When repacking a bag, clinicians should remember to disinfect items with Sani-Cloth or alcohol, or use a paper towel.

Afterwards, the home health nurse should wipe down the interior of the nursing bag with disinfectant wipes. If the bag is not clean, it may be dirty or stained. They should replace it with a new one if they get soiled. After disinfecting the inside of the bag, nurses should wipe the contents with a disinfectant wipe to remove germs and dirt. After wiping down the interior of the bag, the nurse should allow the wipe to dry for a full minute.

Using disposable medical equipment is recommended and if a home health nurse is worried about a patient's health, they should contact the local health department for further surveillance and management guidelines. Disinfecting items before returning to the bag for home health nurses should be done once or twice daily. Also, caregivers should keep items they don't need in the bag out of the way, such as a towel or a tissue.

Careful preparation of the bag is essential for the safety of a home health nurse. A clean and fully stocked bag is essential for preventing cross-contamination and protecting the patients. A home health nurse's bag should also include a tourniquet and a sharps container. These two tools are vital and should be kept separate from the rest of the bag. You can also carry the sharps container in a separate pocket.

Chapter 25 - Head to Toe Assessment for Nurses

Head to Toe Assessment for Nurses

Performing a head to toe assessment is an essential skill for nursing staff. Nurses are in a unique position to assess a patient's overall health. Nurse examiners need to establish a rapport with the patient and verify his/her identity. They also need to assess the patient's feelings and ensure that they are comfortable.

Techniques

Head to toe assessment is an important component of the nursing process. It is the process of looking and inspecting a patient from head to toe, focusing on each major system. The purpose of this type of examination is to identify possible problems and diagnose a patient. Head to toe assessment is typically performed during annual physical exams or primary care visits. Techniques for head to toe assessment for nurses include auscultation, inspection, palpation, and percussion.

Before performing any head-to-toe assessment, a nurse must collect data on the client's appearance and health history. During this process, the nurse will look for obvious signs of distress. General survey information may include a client's height and weight, body build and posture, as well as their gait. Deep palpation, on the other hand, will reveal an individual's internal structures. This type of assessment is most useful for determining musculoskeletal and neurological problems.

A nurse's head to toe assessment may differ from the head-to-toe assessment for a different patient population. For example, a nurse working in an ICU will likely have different patients than a nurse working in a maternal-child home visit. A head-to-

toe assessment requires a different technique for the patient, and it depends on the nurse's goals for patient care.

A professional nurse can share stories and experiences to help students better understand the different methods of physical assessment. During a head-to-toe assessment, students may be tempted to hand out a head-to-toe skill check-off rubric. However, an active learning approach encourages students to consider the items and why they are doing them. It also helps them develop a better self-awareness.

As a nurse, you need to be aware of the importance of documentation during head-to-toe assessments. While doing this type of assessment, it is critical to communicate with the patient and document the findings. You should ask the patient's consent before touching anything, explain your intentions, and ask them how they feel before and after the assessment. After all, they're the experts of their own body, and you should take their feedback into consideration.

Scope

A nurse's head to toe assessment is an essential part of the nursing process. It allows her to ascertain a patient's needs, current condition, and goals. The nurse then documents her findings, forming the basis for her care plan. To help her remember all the pertinent information, she should develop a head to toe assessment checklist. She can use this checklist to perform a head to toe assessment during the assessment process.

The scope of a head to toe assessment should distinguish between abnormal and normal findings. Abnormal findings include respiratory rate changes and a drastic change in skin color. She should also note unusual asymmetry in the human body, such as different rates of strength in the upper and lower parts of the body. Abnormal findings should be noted and prioritized for further examination. The scope of head to toe assessment for nurses is a comprehensive one.

Nurses should use head to toe checklists to help them ensure they don't skip steps or make mistakes during physical examinations. These checklists help medical professionals conduct error-free health assessments and help instill order into a complex procedure. Ultimately, they will ensure that each patient is receiving the best care possible. So, what's the scope of head to toe assessment for nurses? And how can it help a nurse make her job easier?

The scope of head to toe assessment for nurses includes the collection of vitals. However, the assessment goes beyond physical exams and focuses on mental and emotional states as well. Once the nurse completes a head to toe assessment, she is better equipped to diagnose a patient's condition. This assessment allows the nurse to make better decisions about the patient's care and identify any changes more quickly. You will also be able to apply the concepts you learned during your head to toe assessment to patient scenarios.

Benefits

The head to toe assessment is an important part of the nursing process. The findings from this assessment are documented and form the basis of the care plan. Using a checklist can help you remember the important aspects of this process. Here are some of the benefits of head to toe assessment for nurses. 1. Make it a habit to use it regularly

The thorough assessment is important for the patient's health and helps the physician to be more efficient. Accurate record-keeping will increase efficiency, and the rapport between the nurse and patient will improve. Furthermore, the patient's health status can be easily assessed with the help of this tool. This assessment will also help the nurses to get to the right focused assessments. If the nurse has a thorough knowledge of the patient's current health status and goals, the patient is more likely to feel better after treatment.

Aside from making learning easier, head to toe assessment can also close the gap between theory and practice. With a simple recording device such as a cell phone propped against a book, students can record health assessments on a friend or classmate. Teachers can then give feedback on the videos. The process is convenient as students don't need to wait for a simulation lab opening. All they need is a willing participant.

When teaching the benefits of head to toe assessment to students, it is a good idea to include an example of how nurses perform it in the clinical environment. This way, they can see what type of physical assessment is needed and why it is important. They can also discuss the role of psychomotor skills in head to toe assessment. If students have an understanding of this physical assessment, they will be better prepared to do it when they begin their career in nursing.

Using head to toe assessment checklists prevents errors from occurring during physical examinations. Nurses no longer have to worry about mistaking or skipping steps during the process. Electronic head to toe assessment forms eliminate the hassle of paperwork and save time while streamlining the process for patients. Ahead-to-toe assessment checklist provides nurses with vital patient data for documentation and helps physicians translate this information into an effective care plan.

Documentation

Nurses and other health care professionals use a head to toe assessment checklist to record the patient's condition. This top to bottom assessment is used to detect emergency situations and diagnose disease. Nurses often start with the head, explaining the process and involving the patient. This way, they get a comprehensive overview of the patient's condition and can use that information for a diagnosis. The patient also knows his or her body better than anyone else, so it's important to document all relevant information.

Nursing assessment starts with establishing rapport with the patient. Identifying the patient's identity and establishing a personal connection is essential to ensuring the process is painless and effective. Nurses should also make sure the patient is comfortable and aware of what they're doing. By providing comfort and explanations, nurses can build trust and confidence in their work. It's important to keep in mind that the human body is bilaterally symmetrical, and if one part is missing or is disproportionate to the other, further evaluation is warranted.

Having a checklist to document the physical assessment can help students remember the steps. There are many things to check off during an assessment, and a script can make it easier for students to remember. A script can be organized based on the patient's position and other factors, such as the severity of the condition. The checklist also helps students prioritize items and improve self-reflection, which can be difficult to teach.

Tactile sensory functioning is an assessment of the client's ability to feel objects or identify them without visual cues. Performing this assessment may help nurses determine if the client is a good candidate for physical therapy. By assessing a client's tactile sensitivity, nurses can determine whether the client is physically able to respond to their touch. If the client feels a hot or cold object on the body, it may indicate a problem with kinesthetic perception.

Limitations

Although physical assessment skills were not included in the curriculum of nursing school when older RNs entered the profession, they have been reinforced and improved upon by junior RNs. This skill may be lacking in RNs who practice in specific subspecialties. Consequently, nursing managers must focus on improving the physical assessment skills of junior RNs as well as senior RNs. This may be a challenge, especially for junior RNs who practice in subspecialties, and who may not have had appropriate training.

Limitations of physical assessment for nurses

The limitations of physical assessment for nurses are many. The skills taught in nursing programs are rarely practiced in the clinical setting. Nurses' inexperience with physical assessment may be related to time constraints, the lack of confidence, the need to use technology, and the reliance on clinical instructors. Despite these limitations, nurses feel that their ability to use physical assessment improves their patients' care and that their ability to perform physical assessments contributes to the development of effective care plans.

Incorrect assessments are the second leading cause of sentinel events in hospitals. These occur due to the incorrect assessment of patient conditions. An inaccurate assessment of a patient's condition may result in a death. Nurses should be vigilant frontline warriors, advocating for error prevention. Physical assessment is a vital piece of the puzzle in protecting patient safety. It takes years to perfect physical assessment skills. And nurses need to practice their skills as much as they can.

A study found that half of nursing students reported limitations to physical assessment. Some of the most common limitations were: lack of time, interruptions, lack of confidence, and perceived barriers to patient care. These problems may be addressed through further studies, such as establishing a supportive clinical environment and enhancing teaching quality. Further research will help identify barriers to effective physical assessment. And further studies can identify the causes of low confidence in physical assessment.

Increasing reliance on technology and portable health mobile devices could continue to limit nurses' physical assessment. Future nurses must be prepared for these changes and should develop appropriate development programs during classroom practice to minimize the reliance on technology. However, it is important that nurses develop their clinical skills in order to practice physical assessment in real-world situations. But these improvements cannot be achieved without a more systematic approach to nursing physical assessment. If nurses want to improve patient care, they must be prepared to overcome these barriers.

The limitation of physical assessment for nurses may be due to a lack of experience. The study focused on students and not on staff nurses in hospitals. Further empirical studies of the impact of limited influence on physical assessment on nursing practice are needed. A systematic study of the factors influencing physical assessment in nurses is needed to determine the best practices. This study may help nurses improve their skills and confidence. For now, the study only looked at students' knowledge of physical assessment.

Moreover, nurses must use several skills to carry out an assessment. Some skills come naturally and others are acquired through experience. Visual observation skills are important for determining general well-being. The use of senses, such as the sense of smell, temperature, and skin condition, is also necessary for decision-making. Observing symptoms, whether the patient is conscious or not, will be helpful in determining the optimal treatment approach.

Limitations of head-to-toe assessment

If you are looking for a video on the head-to-toe assessment for nurses, you've come to the right place. This video shows you how to conduct the assessment in a realistic care setting. A nurse asks you questions about the quality of life of the patient and then explains each step along the way. Watch the video to learn more about the different steps. Then, get started on your own head-to-toe assessment.

A head-to-toe assessment is a comprehensive evaluation of the body system from head to toe. It should be conducted at the beginning of each shift and on admission. It covers all areas of the body and is important in establishing a baseline for the patient's health. If you notice any abnormal findings, you should perform a focused assessment. In addition, human bodies are symmetrical, so an abnormal finding should prompt further examination. This could signal neurological or musculoskeletal issues.

A head-to-toe assessment is one of the many types of health assessments nurses perform. The goal of this type of assessment is to determine the patient's health needs, current health status, and desired state. Zucchero explains that nurses use a variety of different assessment techniques. During the head-to-toe assessment, a nurse should ask the patient questions before touching them. The patient is the expert on his or her own body, and they will likely provide the most valuable input.

Another limitation of the head-to-toe assessment is that it does not include a breast examination. This exam is usually reserved for symptomatic men or older women. A nurse must determine the patient's temperature before deciding how long to perform a head-to-toe assessment. A head-to-toe assessment can take up to two hours. While this is not a perfect method, it is an excellent option for some types of nursing care.

Another important limitation of the head-to-toe assessment for nurses is its inaccuracy. Nurses can easily make the mistake of assuming that they have assessed everything. But these mistakes can result in a sentinel event. This type of event may lead to falls, infection, or failure to rescue. With proper documentation, a nurse can prevent many of these problems from occurring. The benefits of a head-to-toe assessment are significant and well worth the effort.

The research findings provide important insights about the complex issues in physical assessment for nurses and the ways in which nursing students can improve their performance. Nurses should be advocates of error prevention and front-line warriors who make physical assessments as a routine part of the job. The results of this study will help nurses and doctors improve their collaboration and patient outcomes. This is an important piece of the puzzle for nurses, and the study findings can guide the development of more effective teaching methods.

Limitations of mental status assessment

A nurse's knowledge of mental health will be enhanced by completing mental status assessment. This process includes the assessment of the patient's primary language, physical and mental functionality, as well as their social and emotional well-being. Nurses can obtain this information through observation, a systematic approach, and questioning skills. RNs must be sensitive to patient cues and respect patient confidentiality. Mental status assessment requires knowledge of the principles of asepsis, safety, and privacy.

During the study, the Palestinian health workforce faced a complex environment that posed multiple challenges. They faced challenges in addressing the demands of the local mental health system and cultural contexts, and the challenges associated with unrest and the lack of resources. These challenges, together with the chronic difficulties faced by health professionals, must be considered in the larger context of the collective suffering of the Palestinian population. This study also identified the need to improve mental health services in Palestine.

Chapter 26 - Medication Reconciliation For Nurses

Nurses can easily perform medication reconciliation, but there are several barriers that may prevent this vital task from being performed. These obstacles include: Time and effort; Patient-associated factors; and Low effort interventions. To overcome these obstacles, nurse must know the most important strategies. Listed below are some suggestions for medication reconciliation. Use them wisely!

Obstacles to medication reconciliation

The current literature describes a variety of barriers that prevent effective medication reconciliation. One common barrier is a lack of access to accurate pre-admission medication lists. This problem, sometimes referred to as the "garbage in, garbage out" phenomenon, may also be a barrier to physician engagement in medication reconciliation. Access to external patient histories may make it easier for clinicians to create accurate medication lists. But this research only addresses one of the barriers.

While the process of medication reconciliation has become standard of care for pharmacists, it is not always a simple task. In this study, we sought to better understand the factors that impede or facilitate medication reconciliation, as well as what factors are helpful in overcoming these barriers. In the process, we incorporated a theory of planned behavior to explore the obstacles nurses face and the factors that enable them to overcome them. We found that the theoretical framework underlying the process of medication reconciliation was most useful for nurses who perform the task.

Regardless of the setting, a standardized process for medication reconciliation is crucial for patient safety. However, without a clear definition of responsibilities, a lack of standardized protocols and policies can impede effective communication among healthcare professionals. Medication reconciliation should be a collaborative effort involving all team members. And once it is mastered, it can lead to active medication management. That's why it's important to consider integrating medication reconciliation into patient care.

Increasing specialisation can also lead to obstacles in effective medication reconciliation. Specialist doctors may only consider the use of certain medicines that require a specific level of expertise. The integration of non-medical professionals can limit the effectiveness of multidisciplinary teams. As a result, a nurse may not be able to question the decision-making process of physicians when making prescription changes. For example, a pharmacist may not be familiar with the drug a patient is taking.

Lack of awareness about medication reconciliation is a common barrier. Healthcare professionals may be hesitant to reallocate medication reconciliation tasks, as it is a complex process. Further, some healthcare professionals lack the necessary knowledge about medicine reconciliation and may be unable to implement it in their practice. In this way, the process may not be successful if the workforce is unaware of the benefits of medication reconciliation. The underlying problems may not be so obvious.

Time consuming process

In a recent study, nurses and pharmacists rated how long it took them to perform medication reconciliation. While nurses rated the process as time-consuming, physicians rated it as time-efficient. Both groups considered themselves the main providers of care. According to the study, nurses were twice as likely as pharmacists to choose this process, but pharmacists did not. The reason behind this was that pharmacists and physicians viewed it as a secondary care provider.

The time-consuming process of medication reconciliation is made even more difficult by the fact that nurses and physicians are responsible for managing a complex patient's medication history. The average patient has more than a dozen prescriptions on their profile. Reconciling this information manually can lead to errors. Nurses should also consider the safety implications of a faulty reconciliation. In addition to ensuring that the correct dosage is administered, the process should ensure that the patient's health is not put at risk by the administration of an incorrect medication.

Nursing staff are crucial to the proper administration of medicines. During the time spent performing medicine reconciliation, nurses must assess the current medications of patients, identify discrepancies, and ensure that the medication order is correct. Some nurses review transfer documents and consult with patients and their families, while others simply assume that the medication orders provided at the transfer were correct. Despite the difficulties nurses face, this cognitive process can be done by them.

Medication reconciliation can improve efficiency by streamlining the process. In the past, nurses and physicians conducted individual medication histories. However, a more coordinated approach can reduce the number of errors. Besides, medication reconciliation can be standardized by using electronic health records (EHRs).

Patient-associated factors

Medication reconciliation processes are highly error-prone, complex, and lack standardization. Many contributing factors include limited resources, limitations of electronic health records, and multiple care transitions. To address these challenges, a team of researchers designed and validated a new, systematic process for medication history documentation, MARQUIS2, and additional lists of medications. These processes were used by clinical nurses at five different health care facilities.

A study shows that by using an electronic system, the number of unintended discrepancies decreased by 43 percent. This reduction in unintended discrepancies may help reduce the risk of medication errors, although it is still necessary to implement a standardized medication reconciliation process in health care settings. Further, the study included an auditing tool to track results over time.

In addition to this study, another group of studies examined the medication reconciliation processes at SNFs. In these studies, nurses were asked to complete questionnaires containing 13 items related to patient satisfaction and the validation of the VA medication reconciliation tool. The results revealed that these questionnaires largely mirror the same survey questions but included different patient-related items. Moreover, nurses were more likely to report discrepancies if they were unable to obtain information from patients' family doctors.

Another study focused on nursing role in medication reconciliation, wherein a cross-sectional survey of 14 nurses in Brazil found that many of them had no knowledge of their medication reconciliation roles. However, some nurses were unsure of their roles in medication reconciliation, despite having clinical experience. This study confirms previous findings. In addition to nurses' role in medication reconciliation, a lack of clinical practice guidance has led to a perceived need for further research.

Low-effort interventions

Nurses' efforts to perform medication reconciliation are frequently compromised by errors and failures. The most common mistakes include incorrect medication orders, omitted or incorrect doses, and errors in order entry and transcription. Most events are discovered only after a change in a patient's condition requires medication adjustment. Those patients who require medication change were often hospitalized, or they were in need of emergency care or intensive care.

The aim of medication reconciliation is to reduce adverse drug events. Although evidence of this goal is limited, early signs are encouraging. At UMass Memorial, reconciliation is associated with fewer ADEs. Nurses who engage in medication reconciliation report fewer ADEs. Low-effort interventions have the potential to reduce medication errors and improve patient outcomes. However, further research is needed to determine the optimal combination of interventions. This is an exciting area for future research!

One of the challenges of reconciliation is obtaining complete information about the medication history of the patient. Physicians, nurses, and pharmacists document this information in different locations and rarely compare them. Several studies have examined the effectiveness of low-effort interventions for medication reconciliation, but the most significant research concerns how the tools are implemented. Some have even suggested that nurses should use interdisciplinary teams, such as physical therapists, occupational therapists, and pharmacists, to facilitate medication reconciliation. The implementation of such a team is crucial because this ensures that all involved parties are working together.

Despite the success of medication reconciliation programs in research, the process of implementation is often difficult in the real world. Implementing medication reconciliation interventions in general practice has proven to be a challenge because the interventions require high resources, create confusion, and conflict with other priorities in the healthcare system. As such, many health care organizations have prioritized medication reconciliation for their quality improvement efforts. If implemented correctly, medication reconciliation can improve patient safety and improve patient outcomes.

Low-effort interventions for medication reconciliation for nurses can have a significant impact on patient safety. By improving medication safety, this project can improve patient safety and increase nurse efficiency by reducing the burden on staff. This project can also be integrated into an overall hospital strategic quality plan. By aligning the project with a hospital's quality improvement plan, low-effort interventions can be implemented more effectively and sustainably. This will ensure that the system continues to be a source of high-quality care.

Chapter 27 - Some Common Medication Classifications

There are many different classes of drugs, each with its own unique classification and effect on the body. Depending on the type of drug, drugs can be classified into two categories: prescription and non-prescription. OTC drugs include remedies for common maladies and are available in lower doses than prescribed. Here are some common classifications for common medications. Although not comprehensive, here are some examples of medication classifications you may encounter:

Anti-anxiety drugs

There are several different types of anti-anxiety medications. Most of these drugs are benzodiazepines, which are known as sedatives and work by reducing anxiety. Benzodiazepines are effective for treating short-term anxiety, such as the symptoms of a panic attack. Beta-blockers, on the other hand, are a type of medication used to control physical symptoms of anxiety.

Beta-blockers can help control blood pressure and heart conditions. These drugs can also help with physical anxiety symptoms, including sweating and heart racing. One of the most common beta-blockers prescribed for anxiety is propranolol, which is used for treating social anxiety. Mood-improving drugs, MAOIs, are originally prescribed for depression. They work by increasing the neurotransmitter GABA, which helps regulate mood.

Beta-blockers can reduce anxiety symptoms in the long term. Some benzodiazepines can be found in breast milk. Breast-feeding mothers should weigh the benefits of breastfeeding with the risks of drug exposure. Also, consider whether the mental health disorder is sufficiently treated or untreated by medication. The choice of an anti-anxiety drug should be based on its potential risks and benefits. When deciding on the best treatment for an anxiety disorder, talk to your healthcare provider.

Anxiety treatment with medication is a common practice. However, it can be expensive and requires consultation with a doctor. Therefore, choosing the right medication for your specific condition is essential. A physician will consider your medical history, and other factors such as the severity of your symptoms. Sometimes medication is the best solution for managing anxiety symptoms. Generally, medication for anxiety disorders is accompanied by psychotherapy. Exposure therapy and biofeedback can reduce anxiety. Stress management techniques are also an effective treatment.

Benzodiazepines

Benzodiazepines are generally used to treat anxiety disorders. However, they are not appropriate for all patients. They can lead to side effects such as memory impairment and falling. Because of this, the American Geriatric Society and the College of Psychiatric and Neurologic Pharmacists have developed criteria for the use of benzodiazepines in older adults. These medications may also have unwanted side effects during pregnancy, including low birth weight, premature delivery, and developmental issues.

People who are suffering from anxiety or grief may benefit from taking benzodiazepines to help them relax and cope with their symptoms. If you have been taking benzodiazepines for several months or even years, you should seek medical advice and consult with your doctor. You should not exceed the recommended dosage for any length of time, because withdrawal symptoms can occur if you stop taking the medication prematurely.

Benzodiazepines are habit-forming drugs. They tend to be used for one purpose, but some have multiple uses. For example, some are used for muscle spasms, but these are off-label uses. A physician can decide to prescribe a specific benzodiazepine for a particular reason. Depending on the type and dosage, you may experience side effects from benzodiazepines in any amount.

Barbiturates

Barbiturates are a class of sedatives and depressants derived from the parent compound barbituric acid. Their CNS-suppressing effects range from sedation to coma, and they may cause cardiovascular arrest. Barbiturates are marketed under many different names, including long-acting, intermediate-acting, and short-acting. Barbiturates are a class of drugs that are widely used, but their use is reducing as time passes.

These drugs are typically prescribed to older adults, as their effects on smooth muscle, heart rate, respiration, and blood pressure are much less serious. While barbiturates can cause physical dependence and overdose in older adults, barbiturates are also prescribed for children with a history of tension headaches and seizures. In the hospital, newborns can be given phenobarbital during withdrawal from opiates.

Overdose symptoms of barbiturates may include sluggishness, difficulty thinking, and slow speech. In extreme cases, the effects can lead to coma or death. The lethal dose of barbiturates depends on the user's tolerance and the severity of the withdrawal symptoms. While barbiturates are often prescribed as sleep aids, they have high risk of overdose and tolerance, and can be dangerous when used to treat anxiety, insomnia, and even addiction.

Barbiturates come in many forms, including the sedative pentobarbital (Nembutal), the long-acting phenobarbital, and the anticonvulsant acetobarbital. Historically, barbiturates were widely used to treat a variety of conditions. Despite this, their long-acting effects make them unsafe for prolonged use.

Diphenhydramine

While you may have used a topical solution that contains diphenhydramine in the past, you may be wondering whether you should use this medicine to treat other conditions. The good news is that diphenhydramine is an antihistamine and can be used alone or in combination with other drugs. Common combinations include pain relievers, fever reducers, decongestants, and muscle relaxants. However, before you take more than one medication for a cough, check to see which ones contain this active ingredient.

As a sedative, diphenhydramine can cause drowsiness in many patients. However, its calming effect has led it to become popular in non-prescription cough and cold medications. However, it is important to note that diphenhydramine may increase restlessness, and should never be taken in excess. Diphenhydramine is extensively metabolized by the liver. It is therefore not suitable for use in young children.

People should not take diphenhydramine for sleep in children younger than two years old. Children may be unaware of the effects of cough medicines, and misuse of this medication can be dangerous. Diphenhydramine should never be taken during dental surgery, as it can make the patient feel drowsy. Additionally, diphenhydramine may also interfere with certain medications, such as alcohol. As such, it is important to discuss the risks of diphenhydramine with your healthcare provider.

Nonsteroidal anti-inflammatory drugs

Nonsteroidal anti-inflammatory drugs (NSAIDs) are drugs that reduce inflammation without using steroids. They include aspirin, ibuprofen, and naproxen. Although NSAIDs are commonly used in the treatment of arthritis, they may also be prescribed to treat other conditions such as headaches, fever, sprains, and toothache. In addition to being pain relievers, NSAIDs can also prevent certain types of cancer.

A nonsteroidal anti-inflammatory drug (NSAID) is a type of pain reliever that blocks the production of cyclooxygenase enzymes, which are responsible for triggering inflammation. COX enzymes make prostaglandins, a substance that irritates nerve endings in the body. These chemicals are also part of the body's temperature-control system, so they can have troublesome side effects if taken improperly.

NSAIDs are a class of medication used to treat various types of arthritis pain. Although they are often prescribed as a treatment for arthritis, they can have serious side effects and may interact with other medicines. For this reason, it's important to follow your doctor's instructions for using nonsteroidal anti-inflammatory drugs (NSAIDs). NSAIDs should be taken for only as long as necessary to achieve the desired results. Always consult with your physician before taking NSAIDs, as they may interact with other medicines.

NSAIDs can reduce the inflammation associated with arthritis by blocking the production of prostaglandins. These substances are the body's main contributor to inflammation. The nonsteroidal anti-inflammatory drugs can also be harmful to the stomach lining, causing ulcers and bleeding. A number of NSAIDs can cause gastrointestinal side effects. A list of the most common side effects can be found below.

Etanercept for rheumatoid arthritis

A recent study in Japan looked at the relationship between the duration of RA and the response to etanercept (ETN). The researchers studied a total of 7,099 RA patients treated with ETN, and found that patients who received ETN experienced faster improvements in disease activity and fewer side effects.

Patients with long-term disease duration were also older, had more comorbidities, were more likely to be diagnosed with allergies, and had lower morning stiffness and disease activity scores.

The drug belongs to a class of drugs called tumor necrosis factor a inhibitors. Although it is approved for the treatment of various rheumatic diseases, the drug has been associated with several adverse reactions, including autoimmune skin disease. A 54-year-old woman developed subacute cutaneous lupus erythematosus during her treatment with etanercept.

Although Etanercept can cause side effects, it is generally well-tolerated and is a promising treatment option for rheumatoid arthritic patients. The drug is a biologic tumor necrosis factor inhibitor and binds to TNF-alpha and -beta receptors. TNF-alpha binds to TNF receptor 1 and TNF receptor 2, and is responsible for activating inflammatory pathways. Etanercept blocks both TNF-alpha and -beta receptors, and is therefore highly effective in patients with psoriatic arthritis and rheumatoid spondylitis.

Etanercept is the first anti-TNF agent approved for the treatment of RA. It was studied in both early and established disease and in combination with methotrexate. Etanercept reduced disease activity, improved function, and decreased the rate of mortality. The drug also has minimal adverse effects and a low incidence of infections. Among the approved uses for RA, Etanercept is also indicated for psoriatic arthritis, a related disease.

Sex hormones

There are three main classes of sex hormones, and these drugs are classified according to their function. Androgens are male hormones, while estrogens are female hormones. These drugs act by increasing the levels of the sex hormones in the body.

They are produced by the ovaries and testes and control reproductive function and sexual development. Female sex hormones include estrogens, progestins, and testosterone.

While androgens are the most common sex hormones in men, females produce small amounts. Often, male sex hormones are used to treat hormonal deficiency or disorders of the testes. They may also be given to treat breast cancer in women. Synthetic steroids have fewer side effects than natural ones, and are often preferred. Anabolic steroids, on the other hand, have a body-building effect. These drugs are often used by people in competitive sports to enhance their physical performance.

While prescription and over-the-counter drugs that affect sexual function aren't necessarily harmful, they can affect your ability to have sex. Certain drugs, including antihistamines, decongestants, and pain-relief medications, can affect your ability to ejaculate. The risk of side effects is much greater when multiple medications are used at once. In some cases, a person can experience sexual dysfunction without knowing that they are taking these medications.

Analgesics

Analgesics are medications that reduce inflammation and alter the brain's perception of pain. They are available as tablets, liquids, gels, and patches. Some are available over-the-counter, while others require a prescription. Talk to your healthcare provider about which type will work best for your specific pain condition. You can also research the history of each type of analgesic to find out which one is right for you.

Analgesics have two general categories: non-prescription medications and prescription drugs. Non-prescription analgesics include acetaminophen and naproxen. These are designed to reduce acute pain and are generally not addictive. However, the effects of opioids are more severe and may lead to liver failure and respiratory depression if used incorrectly. Children should be evaluated for the potential for overdose before taking any medication.

While most analgesics are safe to take, some are classified as narcotic or opioid analgesics. Narcotic drugs are habit-forming and pose a significant risk of addiction. In addition to the risk of addiction, opioids can be addictive and should be used under strict supervision. A healthcare professional will be able to guide you regarding the proper dosage and duration for your pain condition.

The two most popular analgesics for pain relief are non-opioid and narcotic. These medications are generally prescribed only after a patient has completed their chronic pain medication. Despite the dangers, non-opioid analgesics are generally safe and rarely cause addiction. Opioid analgesics may cause dependency, which can lead to physical dependence and addiction.

Opioids

Although opioids have a variety of uses and are often prescribed by a doctor, they also carry a number of risks and complications. These medications are available in both immediate and extended-release forms and are classified according to their potential for abuse or dependence. They can be grouped into Schedule I, II, and III, as determined by the U.S. Drug Enforcement Agency. Here's a quick overview of the main categories of opioids:

Opiates are a class of drugs that affect the central nervous system, or the brain. These drugs block the release of chemicals that cause the body to feel pain, such as opiates and a variety of other stimulants. Opioids are highly addictive and often come with a high risk of dependence. They are commonly prescribed for pain management and are derived from the poppy plant, but some are synthetic and semi-synthetic. Common opioids include oxycodone, fentanyl, and codeine. These substances are also commonly abused.

The FDA considers opioids a public health emergency, and has set a high priority on addressing this crisis. Prescription opioids are causing over 42,000 deaths in the U.S. each year and are the leading cause of addiction and death in the United States. Despite this, there are safe and effective alternatives for treating pain. They are known to be effective for relieving many common types of pain, but do not work as well as other drugs.

Antihypertensives

The class of medications known as antihypertensives includes several types of drugs that lower blood pressure. These medications work by removing extra fluid from the blood, widening blood vessels, or blocking the effects of certain natural hormones. The choice of medication depends on the blood pressure level and other medical conditions a patient has. This article will provide an overview of common medication classifications for antihypertensives.

Diuretics - the first antihypertensive - are well understood and have a long history of research. They are the most effective blood pressure lowering drugs, particularly when combined with dietary salt restriction. Their side effects are relatively rare, predictable, and manageable. The ALLHAT trial (which involved nearly 10,000 patients) showed that diuretics and ACEIs were not significantly better than diuretics, nor did calcium channel blockers.

Monotherapy - One option for treating high blood pressure is sequential monotherapy. This treatment method differs from the eighth Joint National Committee's recommendations, which recommended pushing an initial drug to its maximum recommended dose, then adding a second drug. This treatment method reduces the risk of heart failure and kidney failure. But, it does have some potential side effects. The dosage of an antihypertensive drug must be monitored closely, as a higher dose could lead to side effects.

Angiotensin II receptor blockers - These are the second most common antihypertensives in Japan. These drugs inhibit the strong actions of AII, such as vasoconstriction. They also inhibit sympathetic activity and body fluid retention. Moreover, they are essential part of any multidrug treatment regimen. Regardless of the antihypertensive drug that is prescribed, thiazide diuretics increase the efficacy of all other antihypertensives.

Thyroid agents

Thyroid drugs can be classified into two categories: hypothyroidism and hyperthyroidism. Hypothyroidism is the symptom of overactive thyroid glands. Thyroid drugs are used to suppress the production of thyroid hormones. Both hypothyroidism and hyperthyroidism can be effectively treated with thyroid medications. Although the majority of patients with hyperthyroidism do not require treatment, a patient may require a dosage adjustment or a change in their current drugs. This can be accomplished with a printable guide to their doctor's office.

The first type of hypothyroidism medication is synthetic thyroid, which is man-made and given in the form of a tablet, capsule, or oral liquid. It was FDA-approved in 2000. Before then, the only option for treatment of hypothyroidism was to take desiccated thyroid extracts from cows or pigs, known as natural thyroid. Thyroid hormones can interact with many different classes of drugs and even individual drugs. The most common drug interactions involve warfarin, digoxin, and certain antacids.

Antithyroid drugs are also known as agonists or antagonists of the thyroid hormone thyroglobulin receptor. They interfere with the activity of thyroid peroxidase (TPO), preventing TPO from coupling iodotyrosine to thyroid hormones. Despite the fact that they can be effective, these medications can cause significant side effects in patients. However, the long-term effect is often worth the risk.

Drug classifications are based on potential medical uses

Drug classifications are based on several factors, including the chemical composition of the drug, its intended medical use, and the grouping of similar drugs. The goal is to make each drug as safe as possible while ensuring that it serves its intended medical purpose. Classifications help patients understand the benefits and risks of a particular drug. For example, one class may affect the actions of another drug, making the latter less effective or creating a different set of side effects.

Drugs are classified according to their potential medical uses and abuse risks. Although Congress did not specify what constitutes abuse in the Controlled Substances Act, federal agencies typically define abuse as any use that can cause harm to a person or society. Drugs classified as "abused" are likely to be misused or abused, and the FDA requires these drugs to go through clinical trials before they can enter the market.

There are five schedules for drugs. Each schedule has different levels of abuse and potential medical use. Usually, a drug falls into one of these categories if it can be used for medical purposes and has no abuse potential. Drug classifications can be confusing, but it is important to remember that the law only requires drugs that are not illegal to be classified as such. For example, anabolic steroids and ketamine are both listed as Schedule III drugs. Meanwhile, valium, Ativan, and Ambien are classified as Schedule IV drugs. These drugs are typically used for analgesic, antidiarrheal, and antitussive purposes. Drug classifications can be difficult to follow, and experts disagree on the standards for what constitutes an abuseable drug.

Pharmacology is another field that benefits from the knowledge of drug classifications. These systems group drugs according to their chemical composition, mechanism of action, and potential medical use. Drug classifications help physicians identify drugs that are similar in chemical structure, but have different medical or legal implications. For example, some drugs are addictive while others are not, and so they often share the same treatment methods. But the same treatment plan might be used for one person while ineffective for another.

The most important aspect of drug classifications is the way they affect people. For example, the classification system has developed for antidepressants that act on a neurotransmitter, serotonin. These medications also have a positive effect on anxiety and personality disorders. A few other drugs affect the central nervous system, including ketamine. They also have a hypnotic effect. Among the benzodiazepines and barbiturates are categorized as hypnotics.

There are five schedules of drugs. Schedule 1 drugs are those that have no medical value and are classified as illegal. Schedule 2 drugs have some medical value and receive more regulatory scrutiny. Lastly, drugs classified as schedule 5 are those that have some medical value, but not enough to warrant their classification. They may have a recreational or medical purpose, but their regulatory restrictions are not the same. In addition to this, the classification of marijuana has different regulations than alcohol and tobacco.

Potential for misuse

The NSDUH surveys include a variety of prescription drugs, including tranquilizers, sedatives, and stimulants. Misuse of these drugs refers to use without a physician's prescription, in greater quantities, or for longer periods than prescribed. It does not include the misuse of over-the-counter medications, such as cold medications. In the latest report, four common drug categories are combined into a single category called psychotherapeutics.

In addition to the common medications, a number of other types of medication may be misused. Some of the most commonly abused prescription drugs include opioid painkillers, stimulants, and herbal medicines. Of the prescription drugs, stimulants are particularly susceptible to abuse, which results in the need for tighter regulations and more effective treatment. However, there are several ways to spot the signs of misuse of any drug, including knowing the potential for addiction and avoiding the wrong type.

Addiction risk

While there is no one single cause of addiction, there are several factors that can influence a person's likelihood of becoming addicted. Drug use often occurs during difficult life circumstances. Peer pressure can be particularly strong for young people, and their social situations can increase their likelihood of becoming addicted. Family situations with little or no parental supervision are also risk factors for addiction. And of course, genetics can influence a person's drug use.

Opioid painkillers, in particular, pose the greatest risk for addiction. The high that these drugs produce may become addictive relatively quickly. And people may become dependent on them, requiring high doses to achieve a high. Because of the intense withdrawal symptoms and cravings associated with drug use, they may require professional help to remain drug-free. Fortunately, the majority of prescription medications are not as addictive as many may believe.

Chapter 28 - What Is Durable Medical Equipment (DME)?

DME stands for durable medical equipment. It is a reusable device that provides a therapeutic benefit to the patient for a long period of time.

It is more expensive than an alternative service

DME is a type of medical equipment that is used to treat or manage certain conditions. DME must not be more expensive than an alternative service, and the item must be at least as effective in producing the therapeutic effect for which it is used. To qualify for this type of service, the individual must provide detailed information regarding the diagnosis, functional limitations, past experience with related items, and other factors. The MPTAC has also reviewed and clarified the coding and discussion sections of the Medicare and Medicaid programs.

Medicare Part B covers durable medical equipment

Depending on your health insurance coverage, Medicare Part B can cover the cost of a wide variety of DME. Whether you need a wheelchair, a cane, or other equipment, you can receive coverage for these items. Most types of DME are covered by Medicare, but there are exceptions. If you're in need of a breathing therapy device, Medicare will usually cover the cost of its maintenance and repair. The cost of professional repair is also covered by Medicare, but most cost is only covered up to 80% of the total cost.

Depending on your specific needs, your Medicare Advantage plan may cover the cost of durable medical equipment. It may have limitations, however, which you'll need to check. Depending on your plan, you may need to obtain prior authorization before you can use your new equipment. Also, some plans require that you use a Medicare-approved supplier. For more information on the equipment that Medicare Part B covers, contact your plan's provider directly.

In addition to supplies, Medicare also covers the cost of certain reusable medical equipment. Examples of such equipment include walkers, wheelchairs, hospital beds, and oxygen equipment. Medicare Part B will cover the costs of these products for you if you have a medical need for them. Your doctor will determine what kind of equipment you need based on your physical condition, the extent of your disability, and how easily you can use it. Once approved by your doctor, your DME will be covered. However, you must pay a Part B deductible in addition to any cost that you may incur.

It is a long-term, reusable device that provides a therapeutic benefit to patients

There are many different types of durable medical equipment that are prescribed for patients. These include mobility aids, personal care items, prosthesis, orthotics, and oxygen equipment. Mobility aids are often prescribed for elderly patients, as they assist them with daily tasks. Other types of durable medical equipment include wheelchairs, walkers, and bath seats. All of these products can be prescribed to help patients with various tasks and are often covered by insurance.

Many patients choose to self-diagnose their medical conditions and purchase their own DME products. This can include a shower chair or cane. Some patients even purchase these devices without a prescription, paying the full price for the equipment. However, this method is not recommended because it might not be covered by insurance. As a result, patients are more likely to encounter financial hardships or have to pay for the products out of pocket.

In addition to the many benefits of durable medical equipment, they also offer a significant financial benefit. The majority of DME costs are covered by Medicare, which means that the supplier will handle any repairs or maintenance that are necessary for the device to remain in good working condition. DME costs can vary widely by plan type, and Medicare Advantage plans may have different rules about how to cover repairs. However, Medicare typically covers a basic DME, but beneficiaries may have to pay for upgrades or other special features.

It is paid by an insurance company

If your employer pays for durable medical equipment (DME), you may have to worry about how to get it repaired and maintained. Although Medicare pays for most DME costs, some plans may require you to pay coinsurance. Coinsurance is a percentage of the cost of a device that the insurance company considers necessary. For example, a policy may require you to pay 80% of the cost of a breathing machine, but only 20% if you rent it.

Many DME items are available over-the-counter. But some require a prescription from a doctor. Many items are available online and may be covered by insurance. You should ask your doctor about specific DME items that may be covered by your plan. To make sure you get the right one, you can do some research online. For example, Amazon shows which items are eligible for HSA or FSA cards.

Medicaid is another source of durable medical equipment. But unlike Medicare, Medicaid covers many types of equipment if they are medically necessary and cost-effective. While the definition of "durable medical equipment" varies from state to state, it is often similar to Medicare. Many Medicaid programs cover 100 percent of the cost of home medical equipment. When comparing Medicaid and private insurance coverage, make sure to look for the one that covers your needs and your budget.

It requires a physician's prescription

When purchasing durable medical equipment (DME), patients must obtain a physician's prescription before they can be used. While some medical equipment is self-diagnosed, such as shower chairs and canes, a physician's prescription is needed in many instances. Self-diagnosis may cost the patient the equipment's full price and the insurance coverage may be limited. If you want to avoid this, make sure you get a prescription from your doctor first.

Most DME suppliers must maintain a physician's prescription on file. These documents are not part of the patient's medical documentation, but rather an order from a treating physician. It is very important to note the appropriate modifiers for DME-related expenses, and it is beneficial to attach a copy of your physician's prescription to your claim to avoid a denial. Listed below are examples of DME suppliers' policies.

Before purchasing durable medical equipment, you must obtain a physician's prescription. The government requires a prescription from a physician to obtain a durable medical equipment license. While some suppliers may not need a physician's prescription, others may not. The supplier may be an individual or a business entity and must have a physician's prescription. Make sure to insert the appropriate legal names on the forms.

It is ordered by a therapist

A therapist may order a DME for a patient, as a means of assisting them with activities of daily living. A DME may be prescribed to help with functional mobility and activities of daily living (ADLs). An evaluation by a multidisciplinary team, including physiatrists, occupational therapists, physical therapists, speech and language pathologists, and rehabilitation nurses, can determine if a patient requires a specific piece of equipment. A person may be eligible to receive DME for home use, allowing them to return to their home, community, or workplace.

It is delivered by a licensed supplier

In most cases, durable medical equipment (DME) is not a disposable item. It is intended for continued use and can include a hospital bed delivered to the patient's home or a wheelchair. Other examples of DME include bath chairs, prosthetic limbs, and oxygen supplies. For these items to be covered under Medicare, the provider must have a regional carrier license. In some cases, the provider is a home health agency.

If you are looking to provide DME to a nursing home or hospital, you need to obtain a license for this business. A DME permit allows you to procure and distribute the needed DME to residents. This license does not grant you authority to procure prescription drugs, but it does give you the authority to sell and lease DME. The permit also allows you to sell and lease the DME to nursing homes.

You can search by Medicaid provider ID or name to find a licensed DME supplier in your area. Using this database will help you identify a provider that participates in Medicare and also search for the specific DME you need. If you don't find a provider in your area, you can use Find Medical Equipment and Suppliers to find DME providers in your area.

Chapter 29 - Nursing Diagnosis

A nursing diagnosis can be a part of the nursing process. Nursing diagnosis is a clinical judgment about an individual's or a community's experience in relation to potential health problems or life processes. A nursing diagnosis can help determine the proper course of action for an individual's care.

History

The first Canadian Conference on Nursing Diagnosis was held in Toronto in 1977. It was followed by an International Nursing Conference in Alberta, Canada, in 1987. In 1982, the North American Nursing Diagnosis Association was formed. This group recognized the contributions of nurses in the United States and used Sr. Callista Roy's "nine patterns of unitary man" as an organizing principle. The group also made an early taxonomy, listing nursing diagnoses alphabetically. Although deemed unscientific, the original taxonomy was revised by NANDA in 1984, and renamed it "human response patterns". Gordon's functional health pattern is the basis of this process and will be discussed in future chapters.

After the Second World War, the United States saw a surge of nurses returning from military service. These nurses were highly skilled in diagnosing and treating medical conditions with physicians, and faced renewed domination by medical professionals and social pressures to return to traditionally defined female roles. They felt increased pressure to redefine their uniqueness, and began to see nursing diagnosis as an essential part of clinical practice. They began to use problem-focused diagnosis as a frame of reference to evaluate a patient's health.

Problem-focused diagnosis

Nurses can make a problem-focused diagnosis of a patient based on a physical examination. This approach is helpful in promoting patient safety. The actual diagnosis refers to the presence of signs and symptoms that indicate the patient is suffering from an illness. It is important to remember that problem-focused diagnosis is not necessarily more important than risk-diagnosis, as risk-diagnosis is often the most important for the patient.

The four components of a problem-focused nursing diagnosis include the label, definition, defining characteristics, and related factors. The defining characteristics refer to the signs and symptoms that collectively comprise the diagnosis. They may also be subdivided into major and minor components. If there is a significant difference between the defining characteristics and the diagnosis, the latter should be chosen. The label should be the more specific, because the more detailed the information, the more accurate the diagnosis will be.

Traditionally, medical diagnoses are made by a medical professional. They deal with disease, medical problems, and life processes. RNs may make a problem-focused diagnosis if they are examining a patient. But the RN must follow the physician's order and carry out the prescribed treatment. If a physician has given a problem-focused diagnosis, the nurse must refer to the patient's diagnosis when making a clinical decision.

Risk diagnosis

In the field of nursing, risk diagnosis refers to a potential problem that has certain characteristics or factors. Risk factors increase the probability of a person developing the condition in question. For example, an older patient with diabetes and vertigo could be classified as a Risk for Injury, or he could be suffering from impaired gas exchange. Similarly, a health promotion diagnosis, or wellness diagnosis, may be appropriate for a patient who does not want to seek medical care. A risk diagnosis is a type of nursing practice that seeks to promote wellness and prevent illness.

A nurse should identify risk factors in addition to symptoms to determine what interventions are needed to treat the condition. They must take into account Maslow's Hierarchy of Needs and the ABCs of airway, breathing, and circulation. Then, they must prioritize the interventions based on the priority of the condition. The importance of risk factors is most evident when the patient is suffering from an uncompensated illness. When a patient is suffering from chronic low self-esteem, a risk factor that can reduce his/her self-esteem is a potential underlying problem.

A risk diagnosis in nursing includes the development of a clinical statement based on a client's symptoms and signs. The diagnosis is usually made using clinical reasoning and nursing judgment. Then there are health promotion nursing diagnoses, which focus on the overall well-being of the patient. A syndrome diagnosis, on the other hand, is a group of diagnoses relating to a specific condition, often a common cause. For example, a patient may have a history of depression, but not necessarily be suffering from it.

Health promotion diagnosis

A health promotion diagnosis is a clinical judgment of a client's readiness to change their behavior to promote their own wellbeing. The diagnosis takes into account factors that can affect a person's risk of developing a specific health condition, as well as the client's own motivation to change those behaviors. Health promotion diagnosis may exist at the individual, family, group, or community level. These factors may include the age of the client and his or her family.

Related factors show a pattern of relationship between a health-promotion diagnosis and the variables that can contribute to that diagnosis. For example, an impaired gas exchange nursing diagnosis may have several defining characteristics, including a person's age, skin color, and the presence of a headache upon awakening. Related factors may include environmental, physiological, psychological, chemical, or social elements. These factors may not be directly measurable. Health promotion diagnosis is useful in determining the most effective course of treatment, but may not be applicable to every patient.

Nursing diagnosis plays a role in health promotion by helping nurses to organize their knowledge and clinical judgment in community practice. Diagnosing a client's symptoms and responding to life events are key elements of nursing care. Nursing diagnoses include problem-focused, health promotion-focused, and syndrome-focused approaches. The latter is the most common, but may not be appropriate for every patient. There are several differences between these types of nursing diagnoses, but they all have the same purpose: to promote a person's well-being.

Enhanced Readiness for Health Promotion and Risk for Falls are the two most important categories of health promotion diagnosis in nursing. These two diagnoses are closely linked by the risk of falling. These factors are critical for the patient's safety and can lead to injury. Whether or not a client is ready to fall depends on the situation, but the diagnosis must be made in a systematic manner. A nurse may use a single diagnosis or a combined set of diagnoses.

Errors in data collection and interpretation are significant factors in the production of an accurate nursing diagnosis. The data may be incomplete, inaccurate, or not valid enough. The clinician may also use an inappropriate diagnosis based on bias and other factors. These errors may also result in an inability to identify the most appropriate interventions. Incorrect diagnosis can lead to errors in data analysis and interpretation. The best way to address these problems is to adopt an objective attitude and validate the data in multiple ways.

Syndrome

A nursing diagnosis statement, also called a syndrome, refers to a group of related diagnoses. These diagnoses are usually associated with similar clinical behaviors, i.e., similar signs and symptoms, but with different causes. For example, rape trauma syndrome is characterized by disturbed sleep patterns, anger, and genital discomfort, while relocation stress syndrome is characterized by an impaired ability to interpret environmental cues. All of these syndromes involve heightened nursing care needs and are often the result of stressful circumstances.

Nursing diagnoses are classified by NANDA based on their defining characteristics. The first category is problem focused diagnoses, which are based on specific signs or symptoms. The second category is a risk diagnosis, which is based on certain factors or defining characteristics. A nursing diagnosis can have many defining characteristics, which means that it is important to distinguish between these two groups. In order to determine the most appropriate nursing care, a nurse must be trained in multiple categories.

A nursing diagnosis is a clinical judgment developed by a nurse based on their physical assessment of the patient. This diagnosis is likely to change as nursing care is provided. However, evidence-based research has helped nurse diagnose the most effective nursing care plans. A nursing diagnosis is a critical component of nursing care. It enables the nurse to develop a nursing care plan based on measurable outcomes. In addition, a nursing diagnosis can help to guide the development of the best care plan for a patient.

Developing a nursing diagnosis

The process of developing a nursing diagnosis requires an understanding of the various parts of the statement. The problem statement describes the current health problem of the patient and its etiology communicates the causes or conditions that lead to the condition. Developing a nursing diagnosis is also crucial for identifying the risk factors of the patient, which increase his or her vulnerability to health problems. The following steps can help you develop a nursing diagnosis.

First, the nurse must conduct an assessment. The assessment will provide cues to help her or him decide on the best course of action. The cues are applied in a decision-making process to establish a specific nursing diagnosis. The nurse then consults the NANDA list of nursing diagnoses to determine the etiology of the condition. A nursing diagnosis will have a problem statement, defining characteristics, and possible interventions.

Developing a nursing diagnosis can be both simple and difficult. A nursing diagnosis can be problem-focused or risk-focused. A problem-focused diagnosis is based on the signs and symptoms of the patient, and is the simplest to develop. A risk-focused diagnosis, on the other hand, takes clinical judgment and reasoning to determine which patient risks have to be managed. In either case, it's imperative to consider the patient's risk factors.

A nursing diagnosis defines a medical condition or disease and is an important part of the nursing process. It defines the nursing response to that diagnosis. As a nurse, you are responsible for choosing the most appropriate diagnosis, as well as the outcome of care. There are several types of nursing diagnosis statements, including clinical and functional. Once you've determined which type is right for the patient, you can move on to the next step. And remember: the more accurate your diagnosis, the better the care plan can be!

Chapter 30 - Nursing Interventions

The term "Nursing Interventions" refers to a system of care classifications. Each classification describes the activities that a nurse performs during the planning stage of a nursing care plan. The following article will discuss some of the most important nursing interventions and explain why they are crucial. It will also show why collaboration is so important when implementing nursing care plans. Here are three common types of nursing interventions:

Physiological nursing interventions

Physiological nursing interventions focus on the physical needs of a patient. In other words, they take special care of the patient's needs and make sure that they stay healthy. Another category of nursing interventions is safety nursing, which aims to prevent injuries. Some examples of safety nursing interventions are IV fluids for dehydrated patients and procedures that prevent falls. They are all beneficial to the patient's health. But, which is best? Which nursing interventions should you consider performing?

Physiological nursing interventions are a combination of basic and complex skills that are conducted several times per day. They can range from simple tasks like answering patients' questions and helping them conserve energy to more complex skills such as monitoring oxygen levels and administering medications. For more complex interventions, a nurse may recommend therapy that involves a team of professionals. However, nurses must remember that physical care is not the only form of nursing care. Physiological nursing interventions are an integral part of health care.

Observation is essential to a nurse's job. This activity involves collecting information through the use of the five senses - sight, hearing, smell, and taste. The information gathered from observation is related to a patient's appearance, functioning, and primary relationships. Nurses observe using their five senses. While performing these assessments, they make sure to check the information obtained. It is also important to verify the information obtained from the patient.

Physiological nursing interventions are not always easy to perform. They may involve complex medical tasks, such as the insertion of an IV line. They require cognitive, technical, and interpersonal skills to ensure the success of their interventions. Cognitive skills are also known as intellectual skills, such as problem-solving, decision-making, critical thinking, clinical reasoning, creativity, and more. The ability to assess a patient's physical and emotional state is essential for a nurse to perform physiological nursing interventions.

Physiological nursing interventions can also be classified into community or family-based. These involve actions that affect the whole family. For instance, a community nurse can help a patient quit smoking by providing support for the family. In a community nursing intervention, a nurse can educate a patient's family members about the disease. A health-system nurse may assist the patient in navigating the health care system, including maintaining the cleanliness of the hospital environment.

Safety nursing interventions are important for patient safety and well-being. Nurses can prevent injuries and educate patients on when and how to call for help. These nursing interventions go beyond fixing a patient's illness or injury. They care for their patient on every level-physically, mentally, emotionally, and socially. They are the primary caregivers and may have a lasting impact on the patient. There are many ways to make a patient's life better, and safety nursing interventions can help you do just that.

Safety nursing interventions

Nursing interventions aim to promote and maintain patient safety and prevent further harm. They take many forms, ranging from education to bed positioning. For example, a nurse may educate a patient on postoperative care, which includes using a walker safely after hip replacement. She may also show a patient how to use alarms to avoid falls and show them how to find their way back to their room if they become disoriented. Ultimately, safety nursing interventions benefit both patients and healthcare providers.

Healthcare-related injuries have an enormous impact on patient health and well-being. One in 10 patients suffers an adverse event while 134 million people die each year from unintentional care. In the U.S. alone, the social costs of patient harm are estimated at one to two trillion dollars a year. Nursing is an integral part of patient care and plays an important role in implementing favorable injury prevention programs. In fact, more than half of all deaths in hospitals and healthcare facilities are related to patient harm.

Safety nursing interventions vary by setting and situation. Physiological nursing interventions focus on the patient's physical needs, such as administering IV fluids if they are dehydrated. Other examples of safety nursing interventions include teaching patients how to use a walker or shower safely. In hospitals and clinics, safety education is vital for patients, who may not be able to use these tools effectively without assistance. These interventions can also help prevent falls and maintain patient safety.

Nurse staffing ratios and patient safety are closely related. Increased workloads increase risk of patient harm. For example, a 2011 PSNet Classic study found a strong correlation between increased patient turnover and mortality. To ensure adequate nurse staffing, management and nursing must coordinate well to set adequate ratios of nurses to patients. Nursing staffing ratios depend on patient acuity, turnover, and settings of care. However, it is important to note that these ratios are often not legally mandated.

Aside from patient care, safety nursing interventions can benefit family members, especially the primary patient. For example, teaching new mothers how to recover safely in the hospital also benefits the family members of the primary patient. Other safety nursing interventions include teaching family members to care for patients and prevent falls. The interventions should be detailed in a Word document, and should include a brief description of the client's medical history and medications. Safety nursing interventions can save lives, especially if they are implemented promptly.

Many safety nurses are concerned about interruptions and errors. The risk of errors increases with increased nurse-to-patient ratios. Additionally, the high-intensity nature of their work makes nursing staff more susceptible to errors. The human factors engineering model posits that a nurse's work environment must be conducive to efficient performance of complex tasks. In addition, interruptions and equipment failures can disrupt nurses' ability to safely perform their tasks.

Collaborative nursing interventions

The aim of this study was to investigate the effects of collaborative nursing interventions on nurse-doctor collaboration. The authors referred to the Cochrane Database of Systematic Reviews to identify studies of the effectiveness of nursing interventions. MEDLINE, a database of articles published up to October 1999, also provided abstracts of relevant studies. These included randomised trials, controlled before-and-after studies, and interrupted time series. The interventions were implemented in a healthcare setting to improve the collaboration between medical staff and nurses who share patient care.

The first step in collaborative nursing interventions is to define what constitutes a nursing intervention. It is an activity that requires the physician's order and other medical professionals' input. The second step involves collaborating with other members of the health care team. Both types of nursing interventions require a team approach, and collaboration between health care professionals is vital to the outcome. Nursing interventions fall under two broad categories: interdependent nursing interventions and dependent nursing interventions.

The third category is a problem-solving collaborative, in which nurses work with other health care providers to solve a patient's problem. Such a collaborative problem might involve hemorrhage, infection, or paralysis. Collaborative nursing interventions also involve physician-prescribed medical and allied health services to address the patient's condition. Once the collaborative problem-solving team has identified the underlying cause of the problem, they can then design a care plan that will address the specific needs of the patient.

Another type of collaborative intervention is the multidisciplinary team approach. This approach involves team members from different disciplines, such as physical therapists, nurses, and physicians. A nursing intervention may be independent or dependent, depending on the involvement of other health professionals. An interdependent nursing intervention involves the nurse's input and guidance, while an independent intervention requires the physician's prescription and supervision. If there are multiple disciplines involved, the collaborative intervention is most effective.

When identifying priorities, nurses must consider the client's health values and priorities. Then they need to involve the client in the process and develop goals for each priority. These goals describe what the nurse hopes to achieve with the intervention. Not only do they serve as a guide for planning interventions, they also serve as criteria for evaluating progress and provide motivation for both the nurse and the client. Once the goals are set, the collaborative nursing process can begin.

Patient Education

Another type of intervention involves patient education. Nurses also help patients' families understand their condition and the importance of following their doctor's orders. These interventions often include teaching family members how to implement their own treatment plans and maintain a patient's health after discharge. Collaborative nursing interventions can be beneficial in many ways, but their most common purpose is to promote the well-being of the patient. RN actions may prevent injuries by helping to reduce the risk of accidents.

Interdependent interventions are agreed upon by all parties involved

There are two types of nursing interventions - interdependent and independent. Typically, interdependent interventions require the guidance of several medical professionals. The nursing interventions that are dependent on the other two are not acceptable in the healthcare setting. The aim of an interdependent nursing intervention must be clearly defined and agreed upon by all parties involved. In the case of an interdependent intervention, the nurses and other health care professionals agree on the goals and the interventions.

Independent interventions are performed without a doctor's order

An independent nursing intervention is an action that a nurse can perform on their own without the need for a physician's order. Such interventions are a critical part of any treatment plan, and can include anything from medication adherence to educating patients on how to properly use their medications. By contrast, dependent nursing interventions require a physician's direct order and must be performed under the direction of a physician or advanced practice nurse.

A nurse may perform independent nursing interventions in a variety of settings. Nurses may perform these activities in accordance with their professional judgment and clinical expertise. They may consult with other health care professionals in order to determine whether the intervention is safe, effective, or appropriate for the patient. These decisions may depend on a variety of factors, including the patient's values, cultural beliefs, and religious beliefs. In general, nurses should be guided by their knowledge, skills, and abilities to provide care to patients in any situation.

There are two types of nursing interventions: direct care and indirect care. The former is performed on behalf of the client, while the latter involves the physician performing the intervention. Direct care interventions include patient teaching and emotional support. The latter involves providing physical care. A physician's order can also be indirect or standing. During the course of the intervention, the nurse will consult with other healthcare professionals or prescribe a course of action.

Promoting Health and Wellness

Community nurses are integral components of a public health system. Community health nurses help coordinate health screening programs and interventions for residents in a defined geographical area. They also advocate for underserved groups and take an active role in public health crises. They collect public health and social and behavioral data and monitor the effects of prominent health trends and issues. These nurses can also provide education on a specific health issue, such as smoking and alcohol abuse, through educational programs and health screenings.

A key part of community nursing is health equity. As a nurse, you can identify disparities and strive to make them disappear. You're not alone in this endeavor - there are many people who suffer from various illnesses, and health equity is a key component of this. The right kind of training and additional resources will improve the quality of patient care and ensure a higher patient satisfaction.

The American Nurses Association (ANA) has a position statement on health promotion and disease prevention. The report outlines evidence-based recommendations, promoting a healthy environment for all Americans and advocating for policies to address health disparities. These recommendations are part of the National Prevention Strategy. The ANA is committed to supporting health promotion and disease prevention in communities throughout the country.

Chapter 31 - Psychomotor Skills for Nurses

It is not enough for nurses to have knowledge, but be able to perform certain psychomotor skills to help with patient care. The following are just some of the common psychomotor skills that nurses must be able to perform competently and confidently in home health:

VITAL SIGNS/LAB:

- Taking Vital Signs which include:

- Blood pressure measurement with a sphygmomanometer

- Taking heart rate per minute

- Taking respiratory rate

- Temperature checks and being able to convert Celcius to Farhenheit

- Pain assessment using PQRST or OLDCART

- Glucometer use to measure blood glucose levels via finger stick (more recently knowledge of how to use Freestyle Libre for continuous blood sugar monitoring)

- Insulin administration and teaching

- Diabetic foot care

- Venipuncture for labs

- IV insertion and management

RESPIRATORY:

- Oxygen use

- Nebulizer use

- Tracheostomy care
- Mechanical ventilator care
- Apnea monitoring (CPAP/BIPAP)
- Pharyngeal suction
- Inhaler use
- Incentive spirometry

CARDIO:

- Nitroglycerine use
- CPR/BLS

NUERO:

- LOC assessment
- Cranial Nerves assessment
- Pupillary dilation assessment (PERRLA)
- Aphasia care
- Seizure precaution,
- Mini mental status exam (MMSE)

GI:

- NG tube insertion and care
- Ostomy care and irrigation
- Gastrostomy Tube (GT) care and feedings
- Jackson Pratt (JP) drain care and feedings
- Impaction removal
- Eenema administration

- Ileostomy care
- Nasopharyngeal and oropharyngeal suctioning

SKIN:

- Sterile dressing change (ie PICC dressings, MIDLINE dressings, Central lines, etc)
- Wet to dry dressing
- Decubitus/pressure ulcer care
- Wound vac
- Hemovac

GU:

- Foley insertion and care
- Suprapubic cystostomy care
- Urostomy care, condom catheter care
- In-and-out catheter
- Catheter irrigation

MUSCLE:

- TED hose
- TKA care
- Total hip replacement care
- Cast assessment and care
- Hoyer lift use

MED ADMIN:

- Various routes of administration:
- Oral

- Rectal

- Intramuscular (IM)

- Subcutaneous (SQ, SubQ)

- Peripheral Intravenous (IV)

- Hickman broviac (central lines)

- Port-a-caths

- PICC lines

- TPN

- Enteral feedings

- Chemotherapy

- IV pumps

- Ear, eye, nose drops

- Suppositories

Tip: For a good video reference, go to MedBridge.com (requires a yearly subscription) for a great database of video of psychomotor skills and explanations for home health nurses. MedBridge.com is a highly recommended resources for various skills that nurses need to competently care for patients.

Practice Makes Perfect

There are factors that affect nurses' psychomotor skills and the ways in which they can improve them. This includes knowledge gap, barriers to learning, and lack of basic resources in the clinical environment. After looking at these factors, we can begin to formulate a plan for improving nurses' psychomotor skills. Repetition is the mother of learning, and the more the nurse repeats these skills in various circumstances, the better and faster they will perform these skills.

Methods of teaching

To teach nurses the essential skills needed for patient care, a variety of methods are used. Demonstrations and simulations are two common ways to teach patients the skills they will need. These approaches are both effective for teaching problem-solving skills and independent thinking. Simulations can also be beneficial for teaching complex information because they help patients relate the information to their own experiences. Lastly, one-on-one discussions are another effective method of teaching psychomotor skills.

One method that has gained popularity for teaching nurse psychomotor skills is video. There are now studies examining the effectiveness of video as a teaching method. Using videos to teach students can help student nurses to develop their clinical skills, according to a recent systematic review. The review searched PubMed, CINAHL, MEDLINE, and EMBASE to identify articles related to the use of video in nursing education. The researchers found that student nurses improved clinical performance when they were exposed to video.

In another case, a patient's poor health literacy prevented him from reading a handout about myocardial infarction. The nurse identified this patient as having poor functional and health literacy. She could impart better teaching to the patient by using the term "heart attack" instead of "myocardial infarction." A nurse could also use the word "heart attack" instead of "myocardia infarction," and extend the time of the teaching session with regular breaks. In addition, she could assign elaborate reading materials to improve the patient's comprehension.

Barriers to learning

During nursing education, the focus is on developing clinician competency. Developing skills in this area requires knowledge of basic science and performance principles, as well as specific dexterity and strength. Learning these skills requires deliberate practice on real people. However, barriers to nursing students' learning of psychomotor skills often hinder their progress. In this article, we will examine some common obstacles. Learners of nursing skills must be aware of these obstacles.

In addition, lack of social support may inhibit motivation and limit practice of new skills. Social and cultural differences may also serve as barriers. On the nurse's end, time constraints and multiple competing demands may hinder the educational process. The role of the professional nurse is not prioritized in the nursing field due to staffing issues and perceptions of educational efforts. A nurse's lack of self-confidence in the ability to teach patients new skills can also be a barrier.

Many nurses are unaware of the importance of patient education. Often, they do not perceive education to improve patient care and therefore, fail to learn these skills. Further, nurses often do not feel interested in this aspect of nursing education. Further, the noneffective exposure to this environment may contribute to students' dropout. Some nurses have even left the profession because of this. Insufficiency of time and money may also contribute to nursing students' poor education.

Knowledge gap

Most nurses agree that they do not receive adequate practice while studying and that this lack of practice is the reason why they feel unsure of their abilities to apply their newly acquired knowledge. Fortunately, research on the knowledge-practice gap suggests that the best way to endow students with these skills is through on-the-job training. By observing the nurse perform a task, the educator can gauge whether further learning is needed.

The gap between theoretical knowledge and actual practice is one of the greatest challenges in nursing education. The knowledge and skills acquired in education programs are incomparable to what the novice nurse needs to perform her job effectively. According to Bendall (1976), novice nurses are unable to recontextualize the formalized knowledge they acquire in school. Moreover, the lack of collaboration between nursing schools and clinical settings is one of the main obstacles to overcoming this gap.

While it may seem obvious, the process of assessment is often the first step in instructional design. Yet this step is the one most likely to be overlooked, despite its importance. Nurses often jump into teaching without taking time to evaluate the determinants of their learning. Ineffective assessment may result in the nurse teaching the same patients with the same health conditions. The information provided may not be individualized or based on adequate educational assessment.

Lack of basic resources in the clinical setting

A lack of basic resources for nurses in the clinical setting can result in many issues, including the potential for needlestick injuries and the need to separate ICU patients from non-ICU patients. This clinical setting also include home health agencies, as most home health agencies lack the basic resources in training and educating their current or new nurse hires.

Many registered nurses are concerned with the deteriorating state of health care in our country, but these issues often go unnoticed. Many changes in the health care system have been made without proper evaluation and oversight from regulatory agencies. This lack of basic resources for nurses in the clinical setting affects everyone, including patients and staff.

Lack of basic resources for nurses in the clinical environment can also result in a disruption of care environments, as well as emotional tensions. It is important to understand the differences between developed and developing countries in order to be able to apply research findings in other settings. Regardless of the context, the findings of this study are consistent with other studies that address nursing shortages. In particular, it's important to note that there are several factors that contribute to the lack of basic resources for nurses.

Besides inadequate staffing, other factors impact nurses' perceptions of the quality of nursing care. Insufficient staffing levels and imbalanced workloads are major factors in burnout, dissatisfaction, and turnover. Appropriate physical resources are another factor that affects nurse satisfaction. This includes adequate physical structures and equipment. These are important components of an optimal practice environment. And while it may seem trivial, these factors can make a huge difference in patient care.

Emotions during the learning process

Emotional wellbeing and competence development of nursing students are explored through the lens of peer and teacher support. It shows that both types of support have direct and indirect impacts on students' emotional states. The findings suggest that teacher and peer support is highly influential on nursing students' perceptions of learning and competence. Although nurse education research is limited, this study will contribute to nursing education by providing empirical support for nurse students' emotional well-being.

Self-conscious emotions can produce negative feelings and lead to self-consciousness. Many nurses report feeling guilty in situations where they could have assisted, and when they are not in a position to do so. They also feel vulnerable when unable to take action. For example, home health nurses highlight the lack of teamwork, which impairs individual effort and the relationship among team members. In these instances, nurses may feel guilty and resign because their contribution was not valued.

The study also showed that learners' emotional wellbeing significantly improved after the course. While negative emotions were less common, positive emotions tended to increase. A significant decrease in negative emotions was seen in the students who reported ill humor, anxiety, and stress. Despite these results, nurses should continue to seek support for their mental health from their peers to improve their learning experience. And it would be better to support them and make them feel comfortable.

Need for more time to practice

Psychomotor skills are important in the delivery of healthcare, but the learning environment can affect the acquisition of these skills. In nursing education, students rarely get enough time to practice skills in the skills laboratory or clinical environment. Psychomotor skills are learned by repetition, and therefore, time must be allocated to drilling practical skills and demonstrating their complexity. Students who spend more time practicing psychomotor skills in the laboratory are more likely to transfer these skills to the clinical setting.

In addition to being a difficult task to complete, students also felt that they were not spending enough time on clinical placements to fully master their skills. Despite this, some faculty members suggested that more time is needed for students to practice these skills. One example is that nurses should allow students more time to develop their skills in order to improve their clinical performance. This will help them become better nurses. Using videos during clinical placements can be helpful in this regard.

This change has global implications for HPE. In addition, COVID-19 has implications for tertiary education, continuing in-service education, and ongoing professional development. While the recent pandemic has prevented the delivery of a great deal of F2F training, it doesn't excuse the need for more time to practice psychomotor skills.

SECTION 4 – After the Visit

Documentation and Communication

Chapter 32 - Writing a SOAP Note for Registered Nurses

Writing a SOAP Note for Registered Nurses

SOAP notes are standardized and organized patient progress notes that were initially developed in the 1960s by Lawrence Weed. Unlike a traditional note, SOAP notes help nurses and other health care providers to easily share patient information with other health care providers. SOAP notes contain four critical elements: Subjective, Objective, Assessment, Plan, and Process. The first two sections are crucial and should contain relevant information about the patient's condition.

When writing a SOAP note for registered nurses, there are two main parts: the Objective and the Assessment. The Objective section relates to how the body functions and the Assessment section deals with actionable items for each diagnosis. The Subjective section, on the other hand, deals with what the patient says. This article will explore both aspects of a SOAP note. Here are a few things to remember when writing a SOAP note.

Subjective and Objective portion of SOAP notes

The first section of the SOAP note is the Subjective part. This information should be the patient's own words, including the onset, nature, and quality of their symptoms. Include where they're located, how long they've been experiencing them, and whether they're radiating or referring. Next, write down the specific medications the patient is taking and how often they're administered. The objective section of a SOAP note for registered nurses should include all of the patient's medical history, including current medications and their dosages.

The next section of the SOAP note for registered nurses focuses on the diagnosis. A nurse must determine the problem or issue the patient is experiencing and write it down. This information is vital for the next practitioner's care. It is also vital for generating insurance claims and proving that you care about your clients. Although pen and paper notes have been used for the longest time, dictated and typed SOAP notes are now becoming more common.

The objective part of a SOAP note for registered nurses should be the most important section of the SOAP. It should include the patient's condition. The objective section of a SOAP note should also include a description of the patient's five senses. Moreover, the SOAP note should address changes over time and how the plan should be modified.

The last section consists of the Assessment and Plan. The last section of SOAP notes for registered nurses focuses on the process of taking care of the patient. The SOAP notes are written immediately after a treatment. In some cases, the notes can be started while the client is still with the clinician. This will allow the nurse to complete the subjective and objective portions of the note at the same time. The SOAP notes are intended to be concise and organized. They should be well-written and contain only important information.

Assessment portion of SOAP notes relates to actionable items for each diagnosis

The assessment portion of SOAP notes refers to specific actions, observations, or other details related to a patient's condition. It should be well organized and logical, and include any observations regarding a patient's physical abilities. This section can be organized in a variety of ways, but chronological order is most common. The goal of the assessment section is to document the findings and recommendations for the treatment of the patient.

The assessment portion of SOAP notes includes the patient complaint, time of onset, and any other relevant information. The goal of the assessment portion of a SOAP note is to document findings and help physicians and other healthcare professionals understand the patient's condition better. A good note can also provide a framework for communication between the patient and other members of the healthcare team, and improve documentation and memory.

Emphasis on Subjective - Subjective portion of SOAP notes relates to what the patient says

The subjective portion of SOAP notes for registered nurses is a vital part of the patient's medical history. It is crucial that the nurse record all pertinent information, including current medications, allergies, and other conditions. In addition, the nurse should note any new information, such as the cause of the illness. The objective part refers to hard data, such as lab results and vital signs. The assessment section refers to the overall interpretation of the subjective and objective information, including new problems or issues.

The subjective part of SOAP notes for registered nurses is intended to provide context for later sections. For example, the nurse may record the patient's chief complaint, but that may not align with the Assessment and Plan. To address this, authors Valerie Lew and Sassan Ghassemzadeh advise nurses not to assume the first complaint that the patient tells them is their primary complaint. The authors recommend encouraging patients to document all complaints so that the nurse can determine which one is the most important and needs further investigation.

The assessment section of the SOAP note should include observations of the client's physical condition, neurological function, and symptoms. Ideally, this section should be short, describing only changes that occur and evaluating the patient's progress. For example, if a patient's condition is complex, it may take more time than a single visit to gather information. Following up on the patient's progress in treatment should include information that reflects the patient's response to the treatment.

The Subjective portion of the SOAP note for registered nurses focuses on what the patient says and what the nurse sees in the session. Generally, SOAP notes should not be written during the session. The SOAP notes should be written after each appointment, and should contain accurate information and quotes. When writing SOAP notes, the nurse should use neutral language and avoid using jargon or slang.

Goal of a SOAP note is to capture specific information about a client

The purpose of a SOAP note for a registered nurse is to capture specific information about a client. These notes focus on a client's physical and verbal behavior. They should be concise and easy to read. Ideally, the information contained in a SOAP note is objective and measurable. Observations, scores from screenings, and other such information belong in the O section. O sections should only include facts and not opinions.

SOAP notes can serve several purposes. They can help healthcare professionals stay organized and remember important information, such as the client's medical history and symptoms. Sometimes, SOAP notes are required by an employer or insurance company. Depending on the circumstances, they can also be crucial for getting reimbursement for work. SOAP notes can also serve as evidence in court. A good SOAP note should be comprehensive, enabling other healthcare practitioners to understand the state of a client or patient.

A SOAP note should contain information about the client's physical status, psychological condition, and general health and treatment plan. It should also include the rationale for testing and what will happen if a test fails. The SOAP should also include information about the client's therapeutic goals, progress, and regression. The information should be accurate and detailed, but not so specific that it complicates the decision making process of other health care providers.

Summary

An SOAP note for a registered nurse is structured in four parts. The first part of a SOAP note should capture the patient's chief complaint. The next section should discuss the patient's history and describe their symptoms. In the last section, focus on their needs and treatment goals. You should also capture their current medications. This is crucial because the information you collect will help other healthcare providers diagnose the patient.

Chapter 33 - Five Star Rating Considerations For Home Health Agencies

Consumers often wonder how to go about assessing home health care providers based on star ratings. Care Compare through Medicare.gov provides this information based on the latest health care provider performance measures. This website is also how you can find different home health agencies and research about them as patients. As a consumer of healthcare, Medicare gives you the power to choose. This brings about competition among the different home health agencies, but this competition is healthy in a free market economy to improve quality of services.

There are three primary factors that affect the star rating of a home health agency, and they are:

- Quality of OASIS documentation

- Rate of rehospitalization

- Patient satisfaction surveys through HHCAHPS Survey

Quality of OASIS documentation is easily controlled by the agency and depends on clerical skills of the in house staff and nurses. The data entered into the OASIS documentation must show some semblance of progress toward improvement of the patient's condition.

The SOC and DC/Transfers - The Critical Time Points for Star Rating Consideration

The Start of Care (SOC) documentation shows the baseline, and the clinician entering data in the SOC must provide "wiggle room" for improvement. They must document their findings in terms where the patient has medical necessity for home health care, such us at high risk for falls, increased confusion, and poor performance with ADLs or poor medication management. Through the episode of the patient's care under the agency, the patient's condition will change either progressing toward improvement, or progressing toward a decline. Improvement is the key in star rating considerations for home health documentations.

The SOC (1st point) will then be compared to the Discharge OR Transfer (2nd) time points. This is important to mention as the Discharge and Transfers should be referred to almost the same. Such that if a patient is Transferred to an inpatient facility, there is uncertainty as to whether that patient will come back under the care of the home health since that patient may stay an indefinite time at the inpatient facility, or be transferred to a skilled nursing facility instead. If the patient has undergone a transfer for more than 4 weeks without being readmitted back into the home health agency, they are considered a Discharge. This is why Transfers must often be treated as Discharges.

DC and Transfer OASIS documentation must show improvement compared to the SOC documentation in order to positively impact the Star Rating of the agency. This is why it is crucial for SOC documentation to have "wiggle room" for improvement, documenting a negative baseline, so that in DC and Transfer documentation, they show improvement. If in the SOC documentation, everything is perfect for the patient, then the DC and Transfer documentation cannot possibly show any improvement. See the Fundamentals Section 1 of this book for the list of M-items that CMS is looking to have improvement for the patient.

These ratings are just one tool consumers can use, but they should not be overlooked. Consumers will still find value in the other quality information found on Care Compare. Using star ratings is an easy way to learn how home health providers were judged and to provide feedback.

Quality of patient care star ratings

Consumer ratings are not the only factor consumers should consider when selecting a home health agency. There are also quality of patient care star ratings to consider. These ratings are calculated by examining data from five measures of care that are important for patient satisfaction. These measures are often considered outcome or process measures, and can represent best practices. During a home health episode, the HHA can make a difference in these quality measures, so it's important to know what factors are most important for quality.

To qualify for the star rating, home health agencies must meet certain quality criteria. Quality of patient care ratings are based on publicly reported composite measures that were calculated using specific questions from the HHCAHPS Survey. Star ratings do not include patient recommendations, which are similar to the overall rating of care. The public report will be provided to the home health agency prior to publication and a person can dispute any errors.

Home health agencies should also be aware of the Home Health Compare website. This website allows patients and families to compare home health agencies and the quality of patient care they receive. These ratings reflect the agency's level of professionalism, communication, and care. In addition, the star ratings can also help the agency attract new staff and boost the overall ability to attract referrals. The home health agency's star rating should be continually improved, if the agency wants a steady stream of referrals. Continual performance measurement and cutting-edge tools are essential to attaining five-star status.

In addition to patient satisfaction ratings, patients should also consider the quality of patient care. Star ratings are an excellent tool to choose the best home health agency. They help consumers compare health care agencies, which is essential for patient safety. In addition to patient satisfaction, star ratings can also help agencies improve their service. Patients who are unhappy with their home health care should be wary of hiring an agency that doesn't have star ratings.

Patient experience star ratings

When comparing home health agencies, one way to gauge quality of care is to examine the patient survey ratings. This information is based on the Consumer Assessment of Healthcare Providers and Systems survey. Home health agencies can use these star ratings as a benchmark for the quality of care they provide to their patients. The official Medicare site explains the different star ratings and how they compare to those of hospitals. Then, look for home health agencies that have patient satisfaction ratings above the national average.

CMS's latest Quality of Care star ratings provide consumers with peer testimonials about the quality of care that their health care provider provides. Star ratings are designed to improve consumer health care decision-making by providing patients with access to this data. CMS measures patient satisfaction by translating patient survey responses into star ratings. Agencies like Johns Hopkins Home Care Group and Potomac Home Health Care are working to provide quality care to patients and give them individualized attention.

Star ratings are the result of survey responses from patients and families. The survey questions were designed to help patients choose the best home health agency for their needs. The higher the score, the better. Home health agencies with more than 40 completed surveys are most likely to have a star rating. But it's not just patient satisfaction that matters. In addition to star ratings, the patient experience is the best measure of quality in home care.

CMS' Patient Experience Star Ratings are based on the HHCAHPS Survey, which measures patient satisfaction. They will be published on Home Health Compare in January 2016. CMS will host a Special Open Door Forum on May 7th to explain the reasoning behind the HHCAHPS survey and how to assign stars to the results. By utilizing the HHCAHPS survey, patients can compare results across states and even against national average ratings.

Home health providers need to be aware of the patient experience star ratings and the CMS website. Some home health agencies do not have enough data to calculate star ratings. However, CMS is constantly updating its website so these agencies may soon have one. While patient experience ratings are a starting point, they are not definitive. They should still be considered when selecting a home health agency. So, before you choose a home health agency, take some time to explore the CMS website.

Patient satisfaction star ratings

Consumers can now find out how their health care providers are performing by reading their patient satisfaction star ratings. CMS's Quality of Patient Care Star ratings summarize key quality metrics to make health care decision making easier for consumers. Medicare-certified home health agencies report on a variety of care aspects, including patient satisfaction with the home care agency's quality of care. These metrics are calculated using the Outcome and Assessment Information Set (OASIS), which is a data-driven tool that includes patient feedback and satisfaction ratings from Medicare-certified home health agencies.

The star ratings are based on the data collected by CMS from surveys of patients and families. They reflect the overall satisfaction with the care received by patients and their families. The HHCAHPS survey results are updated quarterly and are based on patient and family responses to the survey. In general, home health providers are rated high or excellent based on patient satisfaction. CMS uses the star ratings to help consumers compare different home health agencies, while also creating incentives for quality improvement.

CMS measures quality by evaluating the quality of patient care and reports them quarterly. Star ratings are meant to be general indicators of an agency's performance and should be used in conjunction with other quality information. In the case of patient satisfaction, most home health agencies are "in the middle" in terms of overall quality. They average three and a half stars. Higher star ratings mean that the home health agency did better than the average, and lower star ratings indicate below average performance compared to other agencies.

Home health agencies should ensure that they meet OASIS collection obligations. Because the Home Health Compare quality measure scores are derived from these data, it is essential for home health agencies to make sure they submit accurate and timely data. This ensures that the star ratings are accurate and that agencies have a complete picture of the patient's satisfaction. The results from the survey are based on random samples of patients. They provide an objective measure of quality care for consumers.

Timely initiation of care star rating

The quality of care a patient receives can be determined by the time in which he or she is discharged from a hospital. Similarly, timely initiation of care can help reduce the likelihood of readmissions and help hospitals implement quality and cost programs. Home health agencies should be careful to provide appropriate discharges for patients who are able to benefit from home health care. The following are five considerations for star ratings of home health agencies.

The quality of patient care measures will be part of the home health agency's star rating report. CMS will distribute these reports to agencies approximately 3.5 months before Home Health Compare begins. Agencies will have several weeks to review the quality of patient care star rating reports and request revisions of the data if they believe it is inaccurate. After receiving the Preview Report, home health agencies can submit a request for CMS review.

The quality of patient care measures are designed to provide a summary of an agency's performance and should be used with other quality information to make an informed decision. Most home health agencies are "in the middle" of the range, scoring three and a half stars across seven measures. The higher the star rating, the better, while a lower star rating means the agency performed below average in comparison to other agencies.

Quality of patient care star ratings are based on the patient's experiences. The HHCAHPS measures include a patient's satisfaction with the care they received from their home health agency. These quality measures are collected through a survey that is largely conducted by patients. This survey provides the data CMS needs to publish the Home Health Compare star ratings. The patient satisfaction rating should indicate a reasonable variation between home health agencies.

The patient survey star rating is based on responses from the CAHPS survey. It evaluates how well caregivers follow up with patients after they have been discharged. The star rating system also considers communication and outreach strategies. The response rate to a survey question is important because a patient's satisfaction with a home health agency is a key factor in a company's ability to earn a higher star rating.

Chapter 34 - Quality Assurance in Home Health

What is the role of Quality Assurance in Home Health? What do the outcomes look like?What is a quality outcome? Why is it important? How can a home health agency use it to make improvements? What are the benefits of a quality outcome?

Knowledge development

The challenges of QA in the home care setting are unique because of multiple goals, limited provider control, and unique roles of family members. The project has examined the importance of selected outcomes indicators, such as physical functioning, satisfaction with care, and freedom from exploitation. In addition, all stakeholders agreed that focusing on the "enabling" characteristics of care is key. The project also examined the role of the paraprofessional workforce.

In addition to promoting knowledge development in quality assurance, they can also encourage demonstration programs and research. Demonstrations and research in this area should focus on improving existing systems and establishing new ones. Knowledge development must be coupled with knowledge transfer activities such as conferences, workshops, and publications. The QA can establish a Federal commitment to quality assurance in home care.

While home health QA may be similar to hospital QA, there are many differences. Home health stay is generally longer and indefinite, which makes it difficult to define quality outcomes. Further, the patient's stay is punctuated by hospital care. Thus, it becomes feasible and morally important to monitor quality in the home care setting.

Knowledge transfer

The key to knowledge transfer is to measure the effectiveness of the process and whether the desired outcomes were achieved. To measure the success of a knowledge transfer process, the selected person must organize the team, determine the appropriate processes, and document the results. The methods used may vary depending on the complexity, volume, and number of participants. Here are some tips for knowledge transfer success:

First, a good knowledge transfer process should include the appropriate use of research evidence. The information collected in research must be relevant to practice and policy. It is critical to understand the context in which the knowledge will be applied. However, there are several risks and challenges to consider. Improving knowledge transfer processes should be undertaken with the involvement of all relevant stakeholders, including policy makers, various administrators, and researchers.

The main barriers to knowledge transfer include individual, organizational, and institutional factors. Knowledge transfer activities in health care settings are more successful when knowledge about the process is shared with appropriate audiences.

The transfer of research results involves the development of user-friendly materials. These materials should reinforce the key messages of the research. To facilitate effective knowledge transfer, the workbook includes several key activities. It includes creating and synthesising new knowledge. The process also involves analysis of the context in which knowledge is produced. Knowledge transfer also involves the actual activities involved in the process. And the evaluation of these activities is critical. Knowledge transfer is crucial for the successful implementation of new research in the healthcare setting.

The Federal Government

The Federal government has a critical role in home health quality assurance. However, efforts to achieve this goal differ significantly among state programs and agencies. This is because home care programs are fragmented, and there is no federal or state agency that focuses exclusively on quality assurance. It is important to provide a focal point for quality assurance, and promote knowledge development and demonstration programs. Knowledge development activities would include research and testing the effectiveness of existing home care quality assurance efforts and developing new systems. The QA could promote knowledge transfer and stimulation activities, including conferences, workshops, and publications.

In home health, quality assurance processes involve all employees of the agency. The agency is tasked with determining which areas need improvement. A quality assurance process includes all employees of the home health agency, as well as the patient. Continuous implementation of QAPI will result in improved patient care, increased employee pride, and greater job satisfaction. These benefits make it worthwhile to implement a Quality Assurance program. The effectiveness of the program will be measured against measurable outcomes.

The Federal Government imposes limited requirements on home care funding by Titles III and XX. However, states have developed their own standards. Title XX programs generally have higher standards than Title III. The monitoring and enforcement mechanisms are similar to those of Medicaid home health quality assurance programs. In short, QAPI improves the care of patients and agency revenue. But how can an agency ensure its services meet these standards? It can begin with benchmarking results against a national standard.

The QA process must take into account multiple goals and the unique roles of the family. It should also take into account the limited control of the provider agency and the unique nature of the home care setting. It is important to recognize that the overall program for quality assurance recognizes the differences in care programs, the intimacy of the setting, and the diversity of the constituent groups. Involving these groups in the quality assurance process can reveal possible differences in outlook and desired outcomes based on roles and client characteristics.

Measures of quality

A measure of quality can be a number of things, but one of the most important is the degree to which evidence-based treatment guidelines are followed. In addition to strengthening accountability, this type of measure can also support performance improvement efforts. Here are some examples of quality measures.

The process measures in this type of quality measure are derived from data submitted by home health agencies to the OASIS database. They are calculated based on the quality episode that begins when a patient is admitted to the home health agency and ends when that patient is discharged, transferred to an inpatient facility, or dies. While these are not risk-adjusted, they are considered appropriate for all patients and settings.

Other quality measures are based on patient or provider satisfaction. These can be quantitative, or qualitative. The process quality measure may be qualitative, or it can be a combination of both. Process quality measures may also include the frequency and type of services provided. These data should be documented in a binder for quality assurance. These measures should be recorded in the minutes of meetings and QAPI binders. The federal government may adopt standardized quality assurance measures to ensure high quality home health care.

Outcomes are often the most important aspect of quality, but they are the most difficult to quantify. The outcomes are the results of care and the satisfaction of the patient. Outcome measures are also helpful in determining the effectiveness of home health care. In addition to quality, they help identify whether the home health agency is meeting patient needs and improving overall health. So, if your home health agency is not meeting patient satisfaction expectations, it might be time to seek additional training or improve the quality of care provided to the patients.

Data sources

The HH QRP uses a wide range of data sources for calculating its quality measures. These include medical records, patient surveys, and administrative databases used for billing and care management. Although these sources have other primary uses, they may also be useful for quality measurement. There are three data sources for HH QRP quality measurements, which was mentioned in a previous section. However, OASIS documentation is among the best factor for home health agencies to positively influence their quality measures as the agencies themselves are entering the data for the OASIS documentations.

OASIS Data Outcomes and Assessment Information Set (OASIS) is an standardized data set that facilitates the measurement of patient outcomes and is the basis for reimbursement. It was originally developed to measure care quality for Medicare beneficiaries. It includes core data items for all adult home health patients. In addition, OASIS data are updated regularly. The OASIS data is a valuable tool for determining how well home health care services are performing. This is why OASIS documentation is a critical factor in home health agency success.

Chapter 35 - Mastering Your Agency's EMR

We'll discuss lessons learned from hundreds of EMR implementations and the benefits and drawbacks of mastering a new system. In particular, we'll discuss how local user cultures affect implementation, the need for better training, and the importance of knowing why. To help you understand the benefits of an EMR, we'll also discuss why learning two systems is like learning two languages. Hopefully, these tips will make mastering an EMR an easy process such as Data Soft Logic, Axxess, or Wellsky, among others.

Learning Your Agency's Electronic Medical Chart

One of the most frustrating aspects of maintaining a paper medical chart is the time it takes to file and sort data. This practice scatters data across multiple notes, making it hard for readers to find relevant information or piece together a patient's complex medical history. A more organized system would eliminate the need for multiple employees to file and sort information. This system would also improve continuity of care, as multiple health care workers could work from the same patient record at the same time.

An EMR includes data such as a patient's medical history, including immunizations, acute and chronic disease, test results, and treatment history. It can be a convenient tool for health care providers and patients alike, and will make the medical record more accessible to everyone. The ease of accessing the data from an EMR is another major benefit. As technology improves, more health care organizations are embracing this system.

Importance of Training

One of the most important aspects of using an EMR is the training of staff. The benefits will not be realized unless staff members use the system optimally. Therefore, continued education for your medical staff will help ensure your EMR is a success.

The training for all staff members is crucial. The training sessions should be conducted on a regular basis to ensure that everyone understands the system's functions and how it can benefit them. The benefits are far-reaching.

Navigating the Patient chart

The use of an electronic medical record or EMR is becoming more prevalent in health care organizations. These software solutions allow for greater efficiency in documenting patient information, reduce errors, and free physicians to focus on the needs of patients. Pen and paper charting has begun to fade out, as medical charting systems document patient information more efficiently and improve daily traffic and revenue opportunities. This guide outlines the benefits of EMRs.

The EMR allows for faster documentation, which benefits patients in need of rapid treatment. For instance, an EKG can be uploaded to the record in real-time and retrieved by the specialist within minutes. However, the mechanical nature of electronic charting may lead to oversight of clinical findings. For example, assessment documentation shortcuts might default to "normal" findings that a provider must adjust based on the examination. The result is often false documentation, as the provider is forced to document the same things multiple times without changing them.

Patient charts should include the following information: demographics, medical history, allergies, and medications. Additionally, physicians should include family medical histories, immunization records, and developmental and reproductive histories. They should list prescriptions and explain the results. They should also include the number of times a patient should take each medication. Finally, clinicians should include the date of immunizations. These records should be easy to access and maintain for future reference.

Lessons learned from hundreds of EMR implementations

In our experience, EHR implementations are rarely an overnight project. First and foremost, it's important to develop a strong vendor relationship. Your vendor will be essential in providing ongoing support and guidance throughout the rollout. Next, planning thoroughly is essential. Delegating tasks to key team members and creating clear timelines can save valuable time and ensure accountability across the collaborative team. Reference site visits can help you gain an expanded perspective on the EHR implementation process and reduce the number of forms and processes required.

When selecting an EHR vendor, be sure to consider the capabilities and features they offer. A good EHR should be flexible and expand your clinical staff's ability to interact with the live chart. Customize alerts and notifications, including those that indicate missing documentation. Lastly, make sure to involve staff at all levels in the process. Ultimately, a successful EHR implementation will improve the patient experience and ensure high levels of satisfaction.

There are many challenges during the implementation of an EHR. First, there is competing priorities for the project. Key stakeholders must give priority to the HIE. Second, teams had to find a solution to incompatible EHR versions, so they had to develop workarounds. Third, teams had to gain the commitment of the implementation site. These challenges were overcome with strong leadership.

Importance of more training sessions for EMR users

While many agencies are already aware of the importance of training staff, nurses, and doctors on how to use the new EMR system, others are putting off the implementation process. EMR systems are complex systems, so choosing the right one for your agency is vital. Make sure the system will integrate with other software solutions at your agency, meet all regulatory requirements, and be customizable to your agency's needs. Listed below are three reasons why more training sessions for EMR users in your agency are necessary.

More training sessions for EMR users will give users the skills necessary to operate the system effectively and understand how it works. Many EMR systems are complex, and a lack of training sessions can make them difficult for users to master. The key to ensuring a smooth implementation is to ensure training sessions continue even after the EMR system has been installed. Further, consider whether your organization's training sessions will address any post-implementation issues. This is especially if new hires come into the picture as they will be most unfamiliar with the EMR system previously installed.

Training is an essential part of EMR implementation. A successful EMR implementation requires communication, a comprehensive plan, and the support of the entire agency. New software can disrupt agency habits and culture. It's important to engage relevant departments early in the implementation process. Ideally, the more departments are involved, the better. But this is not always possible. A good strategy is to hold a workshop or series of training sessions for everyone involved in the implementation process.

After your EMR implementation, you must consider the training needs of your staff. Do your evaluation of EMR training packages and decide which type will work best for your agency. Alternatively, you can have both user-based training and automated training. Generally, automated training is a mix of prerecorded videos and help systems. The important thing is to assess the skills of staff, nurses, and doctors before investing in training sessions.

Importance of know-why

Knowing the "why" of your agency's EMR is critical for success. Without the know-why, it is difficult to implement a new technology. Moreover, it is difficult to sustain adoption, as users are often locked into habitual behavior and organizational inertia. Consequently, it is crucial to provide training sessions that emphasize know-why-related to clinical work. In addition, these training sessions should focus on the benefits of the EMR in everyday clinical practice.

The "why" of an EMR can be explained in a variety of ways. For example, the initial motivation for implementing an EMR was not clinically grounded. This lack of knowledge may be caused by the fact that the targeted users relied heavily on vendors to provide information and perform hands-on tasks during the implementation phase. This lack of clinical know-why may be generalized across various IT innovations, including EMRs. Further, the vendors' knowledge of the software may not translate to a clear understanding of what it actually does.

We'll discuss lessons learned from hundreds of EMR implementations and the benefits and drawbacks of mastering a new system. In particular, we'll discuss how local user cultures affect implementation, the need for better training, and the importance of knowing why. To help you understand the benefits of an EMR, we'll also discuss why learning two systems is like learning two languages. Hopefully, these tips will make mastering an EMR an easy process such as Data Soft Logic, Axxess, or Wellsky, among others.

Chapter 36 - The SBAR Communication Technique for Reporting

This is an overview of Situation, Background, Assessment and Recommendation (SBAR) and how it can improve interprofessional communication and reduce the risk of harming patients. You'll also learn how it can help your team. You can especially use it after your home health visits as you report to the home health agency or case management or physician about your findings and recommendations during and after your visit.

Communication is especially important for home health nurses as they will most of the time not have any team members present in person. Rather, they will be communicating most of the time through phone calls, text messages, or email. Mastering SBAR is a must.

Situation, Background, Assessment and Recommendation (SBAR)

The Situation, Background, Assessment and Recommendation of SBAR is a communication technique based on the four steps of the ABCDE: situation, background information, assessment of the problem, and recommendation. It was first implemented in 2003 at Kaiser Permanente to improve communication between nurses and physicians in acute care situations. It has been shown to improve health care providers' perceptions of precision and communication satisfaction.

The SBAR technique can be used both formally and informally. However, if you are using the method formally, it is important to think carefully and eliminate superfluous details. As you work with the process, you should consider leaving out superfluous details and leaving the essential information out. There are sample videos available for reference. If you'd like to learn how to use this communication method, we recommend you watch the videos below.

The SBAR technique is a valuable tool for health care providers. It is an easy-to-remember structure that fosters efficient information processing. It also helps to define patient expectations. It is essential for developing teamwork and fostering a culture of patient safety. It was created by Michael Leonard, MD and colleagues at Kaiser Permanente of Colorado. Since then, it has been adopted in the Kaiser Permanente health system.

A recent study of SBAR in the emergency department showed that it significantly improved communication among health care providers. It also reduced the number of incident reports due to communication errors. In addition, the use of the SBAR tool improved communication between nurses and attending physicians, which improved patient care. It also enhanced the retention of information by recipients of the information.

It's a format for reporting

SBAR refers to a form of nursing communication that recommends next steps for the patient's care. The nurses should make a thorough assessment of the patient's condition and make recommendations for further care. They should not hesitate to voice concerns or express their own opinions. If they feel strongly about a patient's condition, they should use the recommendation form to share it with the physician. Incorporating SBAR into a patient's care plan requires significant training, and it may be difficult to change the communication style of senior staff.

In addition to using written SBAR templates, nurses can also use the method verbally. They should convey information in a concise manner, without using long sentences. They should try to keep the conversation short and simple, concentrating on the patient's immediate needs, rather than talking for a long time. The other person should have the opportunity to ask questions and ask for clarifications, so that they can be confident in their recommendation.

In addition to the use of the SBAR template, it is important to consider the tone of the communication. The tone can be positive or negative, depending on the particular aim of the SBAR. The specific aim of SBAR will help shape the early stage section, as well as the mid and end stage sections. The mid-stage section will contain recommendations for the next steps. Finally, it is important to determine what the SBAR format is used for in a hospital or home health setting.

Another important aspect of SBAR is that nurses must exercise critical thinking skills. They should take the patient's current situation, background, and assessment data into account. The nurse should also make a decision as to whether to consult a nurse leader or follow a standing order. Critical thinking skills are key to improving patient outcomes. It is crucial to develop the skills necessary to exercise critical thinking when implementing SBAR in patient care.

It's an evidence-based strategy for improving interprofessional communication

It is proven that SBAR improves the quality of patient care by facilitating interprofessional communication among health care providers. SBAR increased the number of critical patient event notes and improved patient outcomes. The study also showed an increase in nurses' ability to document communication with the attending physician. They also found an increase in the rate of patient satisfaction, working conditions, and climate.

It reduces risk of jeopardizing patient safety

Nurses who follow the standards of practice (SBAR) must exercise critical thinking skills to determine what is best for the patient and whether or not it will impact their standing orders or consult with a nurse leader. In addition, they must consider the background and current situation of the patient. The importance of critical thinking is underscored by the positive effects SBAR has had on patient outcomes. But the effectiveness of SBAR rests on the nurses' ability to apply it.

Implementation of SBAR requires a standardized communication framework across healthcare providers. This framework may be created by establishing a standardized handoff report process or a set of characteristics that are specific to a specific SBAR tool. In both cases, the SBAR tool should be used during patient-related communication to ensure maximum patient safety. It is imperative that healthcare organizations implement SBAR in their care settings. The implementation of SBAR will help improve patient safety and overall health care quality.

Complex problems become simple

First, SBAR is an easy-to-remember mechanism that helps healthcare staff anticipate the information that they need from their colleagues. By prompting staff to formulate information with the appropriate level of detail, SBAR improves communication across the entire organization. Verbal communication is often criticized, but few tools focus on improving verbal communication skills. The goal of SBAR is to shape communications throughout the patient journey and improve patient safety.

Using SBAR is important, but it's vital that nurses know the right information about the patient. In the end, the primary goal of SBAR is to provide information effectively.

Chapter 37 - The Role of Case Management in Home Health

It is important for nurses to know the various roles in a home health agency in order to effectively communicate their report to the agency. Nurses who know the roles in home health agencies can better utilize the agency for the benefit of the patient.

The role of case management in home health is to implement treatment plans that will help patients meet their rehabilitation and quality of life goals. The role of a case manager in this field has multiple facets, and it is important to understand what these different roles entail. This article will discuss the functions of this type of professional, as well as their qualifications and financial responsibilities. It also covers the benefits of hiring a case manager.

Functions

In home health, case managers collaborate with other healthcare professionals to provide services. The process includes assessment, planning, coordination, evaluation, and advocacy. The goal is to improve health outcomes while achieving the optimal wellness for an individual. Case managers coordinate services, consult with physicians, and implement care plans for their clients. They are trained in the specialized knowledge of health care, and work to promote health and well-being throughout the care continuum.

The primary goal of a case manager in home health is to provide care to the patients who may be experiencing a variety of conditions. Home health case managers will develop treatment plans to help patients achieve a higher level of independence and improve their quality of life. Effective home health case managers are trained to recognize and respond to potential complications, ensuring that patients receive appropriate care to meet their goals. Case managers must also be certified to provide care in the home setting.

Coordination involves organizing, integrating, and modifying resources to meet the needs of the client. Planning also involves monitoring progress and seeking feedback. The evaluation is done at specific milestones to determine whether the care plan is helping the patient/client meet their goals. Communication back to the service providers helps them understand and support the patient/client's progress. Education involves helping the patient/client learn about important health topics. After discharge, care coordination is crucial.

Effective case management requires the case manager to work with a variety of people. These professionals work with patients, family members, and healthcare providers to identify needs and ensure the right services are provided. Case managers also educate patients and their families on available benefits and services. When dealing with different professionals, the case manager should be aware of different perspectives and ensure that everyone is comfortable with the process. The role of a case manager varies from organization to organization, but many functions are similar no matter what type of environment the manager is in.

The case manager is the main caregiver for a patient. The case manager establishes a relationship with the patient and their family, facilitating communication among the different members of the healthcare team. Using this knowledge, the case manager can adjust a patient's treatment plan or arrange more effective home care services. Case managers empower the patient and advocate for their health. They also work with other caregivers, such as physicians and hospital staff.

Benefits

When deciding whether or not to use case management in home health care, there are several factors to consider. While the process is largely the same across settings, there are some differences. Case management programs are often not focused on chronic illnesses, as the majority of guidelines focus on a single disease or condition. A case manager should focus on a patient's needs, not the circumstances surrounding their illness or condition. The best way to determine if case management is right for your client is to assess the need and requirements for their care.

Case management is an integrated process involving assessment, planning, facilitation, evaluation, advocacy, and communication. It promotes quality outcomes and cost-effective outcomes by optimizing health and wellness. Case managers provide timely access to important information and facilitate informed decision-making, improving the quality of care and maximizing member insurance benefits. In home health, case managers improve patient outcomes and increase the utilization of home health care services. Here are a few of the benefits of case management in home health:

The intervention group reported a higher level of dependence and overall decline in function than the control group. Earlier, these patients would have been kept in a hospital and transferred from service to service. Case management nurses, however, provided telephone assistance to patients in these conditions, which may have contributed to the reduction in general services. It seems that case management nurses may complement the community nurses' role in home care and improve their performance.

Case management helps home care professionals link their clients with appropriate providers of care. They also coordinate with other health care providers to ensure that the client receives safe, appropriate, timely, and equitable care. As a result, case managers ensure optimal value for all stakeholders. So, when evaluating the benefits of case management in home health care, it is important to remember that case managers should also coordinate with other service providers. And once the client is comfortable with the care, the case manager can facilitate the delivery of care.

The role of case management in home health care is vital for the successful management of care for patients with chronic illnesses. It helps prevent unnecessary complications and improve quality of life for patients and their families. Home health care case managers coordinate the efforts of the team members involved and help patients reach their goals. They use strong communication skills to coordinate the work of the healthcare team. And they provide an excellent environment for teamwork. And they do all of this in the comfort of their own homes.

Qualifications

Qualifying as a case manager in home health care requires post-secondary training. Most employers prefer candidates with at least a bachelor's degree in a relevant field. You can major in nursing, healthcare administration, health sciences, or human services and minor in case management. Earning a master's degree may also be advantageous, as it may translate into increased responsibility and a higher salary. Master of Public Health or Master of Science in Nursing degrees are highly desirable for this position.

Case managers are typically responsible for collaborating with multiple disciplines to ensure that the best possible care is provided for the patient. They are responsible for evaluating and coordinating services for patients who need a wide range of services.

Experience in the medical field is also an asset for case managers, as they often deal with complex medical conditions. Knowledge of medical terminology and procedures is also important. This background helps them better understand the needs and wants of patients, which ultimately leads to better patient outcomes. Case managers often have numerous tasks to complete each day, including scheduling appointments, filling out paperwork, communicating with patients and other health care professionals, and meeting important deadlines.

After assessing the client, the case manager will develop a plan of care for them. This plan is action-oriented, time-specific, and multidisciplinary, and considers the client's needs. Case managers must collaborate with the client's support team and healthcare providers to ensure that the transition is safe and successful. These professionals should be able to communicate with all relevant healthcare team members, including the client's family members, medical staff, and social services.

The process of case management involves assessment, planning, facilitation, evaluation, and advocacy. The goal of the process is to help the client attain optimal wellness while ensuring appropriate use of resources. Case managers need to ensure that reimbursement sources are properly accounted for and that resources are maximizing value. Case managers should be certified and have the necessary skills to perform their job. A certification will demonstrate the individual's competence in the field.

Financial responsibilities

In the field of home healthcare, the financial responsibilities of case management are a critical component of the job description. These managers oversee the finances of their organizations and implement measures to improve revenue generation and streamline expenditures. They allocate funds to purchase cutting-edge medical devices and equipment and provide clinician training to improve the quality of patient care. Home health case managers also work to monitor their teams' performance and incorporate client feedback into their operations.

A bachelor's degree in healthcare management or related field is required for a position in the field. An associate's degree is acceptable but an advanced degree is highly recommended. Case managers must be able to apply their knowledge of business operations and compliance, and be well-versed in health information technology, Medicaid CANS, and healthcare quality management. A strong communication and active listening skill is a must, along with analytical and quantitative reasoning.

Although most case managers are often in the office, a home health case manager must be able to meet with sick patients on a regular basis as needed. Because of the exposure to disease and infection, the case manager is at risk of contracting illnesses. To avoid such risks, case managers must also be certified and licensed by the Commission for Case Manager Certification. This certification can further differentiate you from other candidates. There are many other responsibilities that a case manager can have.

Case managers are crucial to the success of an organization. The role of case management in home health care is vital for both the quality of patient care and the reimbursements of providers. Case managers should receive the necessary training in order to maximize their effectiveness. The Case Management Training Solution was developed by experts to address the most critical care coordination challenges, minimizing financial and compliance risks. A case management training plan for case managers is important to ensure the success of a home health care business.

Chapter 38 - What is SN in Home Health Skilled Nursing?

SN is short for skilled nursing. An SN can either be an RN or LVN. RN visits patients for observation, assessment, and evaluation. Home health nurses also keep journals of each patient's condition. These visits are non-reimbursable. RN visits are required for COVID-19 monitoring and may be provided in the patient's home for the duration of the illness. Home health nurses are often not reimbursed, so they must seek reimbursement from insurance companies.

RN visits for skilled nursing observation, assessment, and evaluation

An RN must make at least one on-site visit per 60-day episode to supervise home health aides who are performing skilled services. In addition to onsite visits, an RN can also make virtual supervisory visits. This is possible through two-way audio-video telecommunications technology. However, the RN must be a skilled professional. For this reason, an aide cannot exceed one virtual supervision visit per patient per 60-day episode.

A licensed RN must make an initial assessment visit to determine if the patient needs immediate care. The nurse must also determine if the patient meets Medicare requirements for a home health benefit and is homebound. If this is the case, the RN must make the home visit within 48 hours of the referral or return home date. It is also necessary to note that a skilled nursing visit is not a substitute for a doctor's care.

Using a 10th percentile value of total visits, the federal government has established payment thresholds for RN visits for skilled nursing observation, assessment and evaluation. For case-mix groups, the threshold is two visits per year. A RN should make at least one of these visits per client per day. A skilled nursing visit can prevent admission to a hospital or a nursing facility.

Moreover, RN visits for skilled nursing observation, assessment and evaluation in home health are mandatory if the patient has a prior diagnosis of a medical condition. If the diagnosis is not correct, the patient will have to undergo another assessment visit. During the assessment visit, the nurse must also observe the patient's daily activities. During the observation visit, the nurse should also make sure the home health aides are able to perform their duties properly.

RN visits for skilled nursing observation, assessment and evaluation in home health may also include medication administration. An RN may administer intravenous medications or administer an infusion. The purpose of these visits is to administer medications. If a licensed nurse is necessary for the administration of these medications, a visit for medication administration will be considered a skilled nursing observation. For other medication administration tasks, a skilled nurse may be required to perform a full assessment of the patient's medical condition.

Intermittent skilled nursing visits involve direct, skilled nursing services. Such visits are generally shorter than two consecutive hours, and are based on the Member's individual needs. A Licensed Registered Nurse or a Licensed Practical Nurse may perform these tasks safely. RN visits for skilled nursing observation, assessment, and evaluation in home health are also called "short term" RN visits.

Home health nurses keep a journal of each patient's condition

Home health nurses are entrusted with the patient's well-being, driving to their home to provide care. Home health nurses often serve as live-in caregivers, using critical thinking techniques they would use in the clinical setting. They monitor the patient's vital signs, pay attention to complications, and follow a physician's orders for home treatment. Home health nurses keep meticulous records of each patient's condition.

When documenting care, home health nurses must remember that written records are admissible in legal proceedings. A nurse's written records include every patient's condition, as well as those related to her scope of practice. As a nurse, you should involve the patient in the record-keeping process, and ask for their input when developing the plan of care. The patient should also sign the journal, which contains important information about their medical condition and lifestyle.

SN in home health skilled nursing

RN, LPN or LVN-level nursing professionals provide skilled care to patients in their homes. Each visit requires the completion of detailed nursing notes. Medical documentation is required to support the skilled level of care, including the patient's current medical status, medical equipment needed, and the estimated period of in-home services. A physician's approval of the RN or LPN must be granted, which is based on the unique medical condition of the patient and overall safety.

Medicaid-enrolled individuals are typically furnished with services through a network of contracted MCOs or providers. Providers must confirm eligibility prior to rendering services. They may require a referral or prior authorization from the Medicaid program. Moreover, providers must follow the state and federal regulations as well as the MCO's provider's manual. These guidelines are necessary for the care of Medicaid-enrolled patients.

Depending on the situation, intermittent or part-time home health skilled nursing services are reimbursable. If the patient can't make the required supervision visits, the RN or home health aide may be substituted by a skilled therapist. However, Medicaid doesn't reimburse intermittent or part-time home health skilled nursing visits without proper supervision. A physician's visit must be a critical part of the patient's overall care.

Unlike inpatient care, participants must be under the care of a licensed practitioner. The practitioner may be a physician, nurse practitioner, clinical nurse specialist, or a physician assistant. The practitioner may be a private physician or one who works on the staff of a home health agency or ALF. A physician can also be a part of a hospital-based home health agency.

Chapter 39 - What Is a Home Health Aide?

Home health aides typically perform unskilled patient care intermittently (as opposed to continuously) around 30 to 45 minutes at a given time a certain number of times per week as one of the representatives of the home health agency. Sometimes they are referred to as Certified Home Health Aides (or CHHA). CHHAs perform similar functions as Certified Nurse Assistants (CNAs) in the hospital setting.

Health aides work alongside SNs such as LVNs and RNs in performing delegated tasks. As such they do not have much liability as the liability tends to go to the more credentialed nurses. Still, in California, home health aides must complete a minimum of 12 hours of annual training, undergo tuberculosis testing, and have a criminal background check. The certification must be renewed every two years.

Job duties

Job duties of a home health aide include assisting patients with their daily activities and documenting any changes. Home health aides also perform some housekeeping tasks. They may prepare meals, assist with transfers and perform light housekeeping duties. In addition to these duties, home health aides may be responsible for providing companionship and assisting with personal hygiene. Aside from the above, job duties of a home health aide can also include assisting patients with their daily activities and administering medication.

Aside from taking vital signs, a home health aide also monitors a patient's condition and communicates with their supervisor. They also teach the patient to take care of themselves and their loved ones. Home health aides also provide personal care and advice to patients on proper diet, housekeeping, and hygiene.

The work of a home health aide requires full attention and understanding of the reactions of the patients and family members.

Working as a home health aide requires that you be at least 21 years old and possess a valid driver's license. In addition, the job requires that you have strong listening and communication skills, and that you have a sense of responsibility and self-control. These qualities are important because you will be dealing with people who have memory issues, cognitive impairments, or behavioral problems. Aside from these characteristics, a home health aide must be organized and have strong organizational skills. Besides, a home health aide must be able to run errands and other tasks along the route.

In addition to possessing the necessary certifications, home health aides should be compassionate companions. Empathy is a vital trait for a home health aide, as it helps establish a strong bond between them and their clients. While seeking a home health aide, be sure to ask questions about their background, personality, and past work experience. This information can help you pair your family member with the right home health aide for your specific needs.

Training requirements

Depending on the state, the state usually requires a 75-hour training course for home health aides, which includes at least 16 hours of hands-on skills training. Training programs must be approved by the state and the Department of Health, and they must cover health-related tasks. In addition, they must include 35 hours of classroom instruction, 16 hours of supervised practical training, and 50 percent patient-care-related experience. Live virtual training is also permitted.

New employees must attend training and orientation. This training may be provided by the agency, but it does not count toward annual in-service requirements for aides. In addition, documentation of training and competency evaluations must be maintained in the aide's personnel file. It must support the training requirements and the annual performance evaluation. The program must also adhere to the guidelines of the Board. If it does not, it should consider reapplying for approval.

Home health aides often spend most of their time with the same patient. As such, they develop close relationships with the patient and become a constant companion. This personal connection makes them a valuable member of the healthcare team and helps them monitor their condition more closely. They also report any changes to doctors and family members. Ultimately, this is why home health aides are important. For this reason, home health aides need to have excellent communication skills.

In addition to providing in-service training, home health aide training programs must also provide comprehensive classroom and supervised hands-on training in non-nurse aide skills. These skills may include taking blood pressure, maintaining a safe home environment, and assisting with medication administration. A home health aide must also be capable of observing and recording in a home health care environment. Unlike nurses, home health aides are not required to complete their nursing education, but the training must include the essential skills for the job.

Home health aide training hours vary from state to state. The federal law requires 75 hours of hands-on practical training, including at least 16 hours of clinical practice. Other states require more training, requiring CNA or nursing degrees. In Washington DC for example, aides must complete an application fee, pass a competency exam, and undergo a criminal background check.

Chapter 40 - The Role of the Physical Therapist in Home Health

Home health physical therapy involves a licensed therapist coming to a patient's home to provide individualized treatment plans typically involving the gross movements of the musculoskeletal system. This specialized service is designed for patients with acute conditions or limited mobility, and is covered by most insurance plans. Home health physical therapy focuses on improving a patient's strength and mobility. It can also help a patient who is recovering from an illness or injury.

Most patients receiving home health physical therapy are referred by a health care provider. The health care provider can vouch for the medical necessity of home-care physical therapy, as outlined in the patient's medical necessity report. In this case, the health care provider will likely state that the patient cannot leave the home due to his or her condition. However, patients with mobility issues may also choose to use an outpatient physical therapy clinic to receive PT at home, although it may conflict with the home health agency they are currently using at the time. In such cases where the patient decides to keep their current home health agency, the physical therapist will provide exercises for the patient to do at home.

Unlike a traditional PT, a PT in home health physical therapy has more flexibility in their schedule than in traditional settings. Often, they are allowed to visit the store and post office in between patients. However, in some cases, they are required to cover another therapist's patient or to adjust their schedule for the day. They also must manage the area and patient load, which may be more demanding than a traditional job.

As a PT in home health, they will be responsible for assessing a patient's care needs and evaluating their level of function. They will also develop a treatment plan and advise the patient's family regarding their condition. The occupational requirements for a PT in home health physical therapy vary depending on the state you live in.

Physical therapists typically provide paperwork handouts to patients and their families of the prescribed exercises they can do at home. It is up to the therapists and nurses to make sure they follow through on doing their exercises at home so the patients and their family become more independent.

A PT in home health care works closely with patients who are recovering from an illness or injury. They are a problem solver and focus on restoring patients' functional movement. Therapists strive to help patients avoid prescription pain medications or surgery and focus on improving their quality of life. A PT is also sensitive to the emotional aspects of recovery.

Chapter 41 - What Is Home Health Occupational Therapy?

Occupational therapists are trained professionals who assess a patient's functional needs and help them learn new skills. OTs are typically mistaken as PTs and although their job functions overlap, they have distinct differences, as OTs focus more on the fine motor skills and activities of daily living. PTs focus more on gross mobility such as walking.

Occupational therapists

Occupational therapists in home health have a variety of different roles, from helping people adjust to new situations to managing the symptoms of a chronic illness. They assess a patient's needs and abilities to develop a plan of care to make their lives easier. Occupational therapists help patients manage daily activities by helping them adapt to the environment and the limitations of their physical capabilities. The work of an occupational therapist can vary greatly depending on a patient's health and ability level, the nature of their illness, and the location of their home.

The most common reason to use occupational therapy is to improve independence. As people age or develop illnesses, many of their daily activities can become difficult. Occupational therapy can help patients adapt to these changes and integrate into their social situations. Home health assessments allow occupational therapists to develop individualized plans for each patient. Occupational therapists may recommend training and equipment to assist a patient with daily activities, or they may even guide family members and friends on how to care for themselves and their loved ones.

Home health services may be covered by Medicare if a patient's condition is serious enough to require occupational therapy. Occupational therapy is not yet a primary provider of home health services, so its coverage rules may vary by insurance company. However, the government does provide occupational therapists with a limited scope of practice. Its role in home health care is an essential part of home health, and is essential once other services have been completed.

Home health therapists specialize in helping patients recover from injury or illness by improving their ability to perform daily activities. Like physical therapists, occupational therapists help patients improve their physical movements. Their job title, however, is more specific. These professionals may assist patients with work or leisure activities, as well. A home health occupational therapist can help those who are recovering from a stroke or other physical condition.

Occupational therapists assess needs

Occupational therapists assess a patient's home health needs to determine which modifications need to be made. Common home modifications include removing falls hazards, rearranging walkways throughout the home, and installing equipment such as handrails, grab bars, slip-resistant flooring, and medical alert systems. Because older adults often have multiple chronic conditions and take multiple medications, they need to be monitored for adverse drug reactions.

Occupational therapists assess the needs of patients in their own homes to provide home health services that improve their quality of life. With their expertise, occupational therapists help patients develop and maintain skills that enable increased independence. Many people have trouble with their mobility after major surgery, or suffer from significant illnesses or conditions that decrease strength. Brain damage can also limit one's abilities and make daily activities difficult or impossible.

Occupational therapists assess these needs and recommend appropriate resources.

Many older adults struggle to perform basic tasks. Occupational therapy can help them stay active and independent in their own homes by teaching them how to complete everyday tasks without straining their joints. It can also address the mental health issues of older adults, such as depression. Occupational therapists help older adults learn how to cope with depression and other mental health disorders, while teaching them how to structure their day and break down tasks.

While there are many issues facing the profession of home health care, OTs are crucial in addressing these challenges. In home health, OTs assess clients' needs and create routines to optimize client compliance with the home care plan. Despite the importance of occupational therapy, the profession is still not recognized as a necessary part of home health. AOTA's Federal Affairs Team is working to improve this situation. AOTA's efforts on the PDGM bill have been fruitful. In addition to these changes, AOTA is also working with home health agencies to recognize their occupational therapy qualifications.

Therapists help prevent falls

Home health PTs and OTs often help elderly clients with fall prevention. Occupational therapists can help patients reduce pain medication and reduce opioid use. They can help improve home safety by removing hazards and recommending equipment and training users to reduce risk of falling. An OT can help clients develop a greater sense of self and decrease fears of falling. They can also provide additional information to help the client become more independent.

The role of occupational therapists in home health is to help their clients learn essential skills and perform daily activities. Because falls are one of the leading causes of injury among the elderly, occupational therapists are required to educate themselves on fall prevention. They should teach residents to reduce the risk of falling by modifying their environment and making changes as needed. This will help individuals feel more confident with their daily activities and avoid self-limiting behaviors.

Home safety evaluations are another key role of occupational therapists in home health. They evaluate a patient's home and recommend equipment that will enhance independence while reducing the risk of falls. Home modifications may include removing throw rugs, installing grab bars, or rearranging walkways throughout the home. Occupational therapists may also recommend elevating sitting surfaces and removing cords.

The risks of falls are complex and can stem from the environment, activity, and health conditions of older adults. Aged adults typically lack the physical stability to keep themselves upright. Women are at a greater risk than men. Individuals with chronic health conditions, recent hospitalization, and history of falls are at higher risk. A fall can also be a result of sedentary lifestyles, a weakened immune system, or other health conditions.

Chapter 42 - What is a Speech Therapist in Home Health?

A speech therapist, also known as a ST, is a member of the health care team that provides Speech Therapy services to patients. They perform their duties according to the standards of clinical practice and work under the supervision of a physician and nursing supervisor.

Job description

A speech therapist (sometimes called speech pathologist) in home health is responsible for the evaluation of patient's care needs and determining a treatment plan that will improve the patient's communication, swallowing, or cognitive skills. This person also evaluates the client's home environment. A speech pathologist also documents the progress of each client. A typical job description of an ST in home health is as follows:

The job description of an ST in home health includes evaluating the patient's level of function using evaluations and basic audiological assessments especially if the patient has dysphagia or risk for aspiration with difficulty swallowing. They also work with the health care team to develop a treatment plan. During each visit, the speech therapist completes progress notes and submits them per the home health agency's policy. As a member of the home health team, the speech therapist administers therapy and guides the patient in the use of communicative devices. They also participate in case conferences and prepare clinical notes and reports any changes to the physician or supervising nurse.

A speech therapist in home health can provide in-home services to people with physical, mental, or cognitive disabilities. A home health speech therapist may assist nonverbal stroke patients in learning to use text-to-speech technology. They may also test the patient's ability to swallow and trial different liquids. Occasionally, they will instruct the patient's family how to prepare pureed foods safely and effectively.

Qualifications

To work in home health, a speech therapist must have a master's degree in speech-language pathology or another related field. Some states also require that a speech-language pathologist be certified and licensed. Other essential skills include excellent interpersonal and non-verbal communication, patient, and analytical thinking. Home health speech therapists must also know the proper tools for rehabilitation. They must be well-informed about different types of rehabilitation equipment and their use.

In a home health setting, the speech-language therapist will visit the patient in their own home to treat speech, swallowing, or cognitive disorders. They will work closely with other care providers in the home to tailor therapy sessions based on the patient's specific needs. The home environment will help the speech therapist work with the patient to get the best results possible. This includes the patient's family and caregivers.

Home-based speech-language pathologists are highly trained and experienced in providing therapy services in a wide variety of settings. They also maintain accurate records and are required to comply with the highest standards of clinical care.

Chapter 43 - Medical Social Worker in Home Health

Duties

A medical social worker (MSW) in a home health care setting performs a variety of important tasks to ensure that patients are receiving the highest quality of care possible. They provide support and assistance to patients and their families, as well as coordinate services such as medication, home care, counseling, and transportation. They may also provide counseling on community resources. For example, California patients with MediCal benefits may be eligible for IHSS (In Home Supportive Services) compensation. This IHSS benefit allows eligible patients and their families monetary compensation to acquire a live-in caregiver or compensate their family for providing care to the patient since they are taking time away from their typical work duties.

MSW also assist law enforcement officers and perform investigations. This may be if there is suspicion of elder abuse in the home of facility. Duties of a medical social worker in home health care vary widely, but they typically focus on the emotional and physical needs of their patients.

Medical social workers also help patients navigate the health care system. These professionals coordinate care for patients after they have been discharged from the hospital. They also help patients schedule appointments, medications, and therapy sessions. These social workers may be involved with both inpatient and outpatient care. These individuals often help patients and families transition from hospital to home health care. Some medical social workers also help coordinate home health services and train other health care staff to provide patient-centered care.

A medical social worker in home health must have strong interpersonal skills, a thorough understanding of patients' needs, and problem-solving skills. An emotional stable, compassionate attitude is crucial. Those who wish to pursue this career should have a master's degree.

A medical social worker in home health care provides comprehensive, nonclinical care to patients. In addition to assessing and treating physical health conditions, the job requires an individual with excellent communication skills and excellent listening skills. Experience in a hospital or other healthcare setting is advantageous, since it helps them become familiar with medical terminology and the healthcare system. And since the majority of home health services are covered by Medicare and Medicaid, medical social workers are well-placed to provide emotional support and resources for patients.

The medical social worker in home health care is an essential member of a medical team. The social worker's job is to help patients cope with the stress and anxiety that often accompany the recovery process. By educating patients about resources available, medical social workers can help them comply with medical recommendations and avoid hospital readmissions. They also educate patients about the support services available to them in their local community. They provide emotional support and education, which can lead to better health outcomes.

Chapter 44 - Director of Nursing (DON/DPCS) in Home Health

The Director of Nursing (DON) or sometimes referred to as Director of Patient Care Services DPCS) is a more senior member of the agency. They are managers of the home health agency, especially pertaining to clinical care, but with administrative and business duties as well. Directors work closely with the administrators or owners of the agency to make sure the business is functioning optimally. With extensive experience under their belt, a DPCS in home health provides all clinical staff with the knowledge and skills they need to manage a successful organization.

In addition to developing clinical care services, the DPCS oversees agency nursing personnel and contracted services. In addition to overseeing patient care, a DPCS oversees staff meetings, case conferences, and in-service training programs. In addition to overseeing clinical records, the DPCS represents home health on various committees. They must adhere to a set of standards of care and adhere to legal, regulatory, and accreditation standards.

To become a DPCS in home health, one must be a registered nurse with at least three years of experience in the field. To become a DPCS, one must have at least a Bachelor's degree in nursing, and at least one to three years of home health care supervisory experience. A DPCS also oversees the assignment of appropriate staff to each case. Besides overseeing the staff, DPCSs must follow state laws and policies. They must review patient medical files on a regular basis.

DPCS responsibilities in home health are important to the safety of a patient. An agency that meets these requirements should notify the patient of the payment source and complaints procedure. They should not discharge a patient without consulting with a physician. They must also inform their patient's legal representative, attending physician, or advanced practice nurse prescriber. These individuals must receive written notice of the fees and terms of service.

Chapter 45 - Primary Care Provider Roles (PCP)

A primary care provider is one of the most important doctors in a patient's health care system. Performing at their highest level, primary care providers improve patient health dramatically. They provide general medical care, coordinate care with other physicians, and develop relationships with their patients. However, this doctor can also specialize in a specific area of medicine. The PCP is typically the one to officially certify the patient for home health services.

Providing general medical care

It has been found that readmission to hospital inpatient care is drastically reduced if the patient sees their PCP within 2 weeks of discharge. This is why as home health providers, you have a distinct advantage if the patient sees their PCP as soon as possible after discharging from an inpatient facility and is the reason why most home health nurses encourage their patients to see their primary care providers.

The primary care provider may prescribe new medications, diagnose new illnesses, or order new tests. It is up to the home health nurse to update the patient's chart in the home health agency's EMR to reflect these changes made by the PCP, and to follow through on the orders of the PCP to ensure the plan of the PCP goes smoothly. The PCP often, through their knowledge and expertise, make the job of the home health nurse easier by providing them the proper plan of action during visits to medically stabilize the patient so patients remain in the home safely and prevent exacerbation of symptoms that may affect the star rating of the home health agency.

Providing general medical care involves the care of patients of any age, regardless of their illness or ailment. As a primary care physician, they listen to patient's symptoms and diagnose illnesses, and work with other doctors and specialists to provide complete care. In some cases, you may work in a family practice or at a doctor's office. In general, though, primary care physicians are the primary providers of health care, not specialists. Some patients seek specialists directly, but this is not the best practice. It is up to the home health nurse often times to educate the patients and their families on the importance of the primary care provider. PCPs are also sometimes referred to as "gatekeepers of the healthcare system."

Prevention of disease

The prevention of disease is an important component of the PCP and goes in tandem with home health care. These services are delivered by a primary care provider or a nurse practitioner. They can address chronic conditions and disabilities as well as the home environment. These services may be provided through a multidisciplinary team or referral to a health care professional. These services aim to minimize negative outcomes and maximize positive ones. For example, they can improve the quality of life and reduce medical expenditure for patients.

Access to primary care is a key aspect of a patient-centered medical home. Increasing access to primary care practices can help control medical costs while improving the quality of care. Many practices have begun transforming into patient-centered medical homes. These practices will involve patients in treatment decisions, hire nurses and care managers to follow up with patients and coordinate their care. This model focuses on prevention and chronic care as well.

A primary care provider's role in a medical home is critical to the patient's health. Medical homes must be located within the "medical neighborhood." This area includes hospitals, specialty physicians, social workers, long-term care facilities, and mental health providers. Often, a primary care provider coordinates care with other providers so that patients do not fall through the cracks. In addition, the primary care provider ensures continuity of care, ensuring that the patient does not experience duplicate care or slip through the cracks.

Management of chronic conditions

For thousands of Americans, managing chronic conditions in home health is a daily struggle. Thankfully, there are many resources for chronic disease management, including a primary care provider who can answer questions and walk with patients through the process. Chronic conditions typically require more intensive care than acute illnesses, and a primary care provider can help ease the burden and make the process as smooth as possible. Managing chronic conditions is critical to the quality of life of many individuals with chronic illnesses.

While many people deal with multiple chronic medical conditions, the majority of time is spent managing these problems, which can be exhausting. Chronic care management helps people with multiple chronic illnesses achieve their health goals and enjoy life to the fullest. The program is also helpful for hospitals, which can react to a patient's health changes as they happen and reduce in-person visits. Chronic illness can be a debilitating experience for the individual, family, and caregiver.

The center for Medicare & Medicaid Services recognizes in home nursing as an integral component of primary health care. It defines in-home nurse care as care coordination outside of the office. It aims to improve healthcare delivery and quality by helping people manage their chronic conditions more effectively at home. Moreover, this program supports the integration of health care and community resources.

Managing a patient's overall health care

Managing a patient's overall health is a crucial aspect of being a primary care provider. It involves guiding patients toward good health, preventing illness, and managing stress. It involves monitoring vaccines and other screening tests to check for disease and provide treatment when problems do occur. Managing a patient's overall health care may also involve working with other health professionals, such as emergency room doctors and psychiatrists.

In general, healthcare professionals have traditionally fallen into one of two categories: specialists and primary care providers. With the rise of the value-based care reimbursement model, healthcare organizations are forced to rethink how they deliver health care. By combining primary care and specialty care, these teams are better equipped to identify and manage populations at high risk. Ultimately, the aim is to improve the quality of care and length of life of patients with chronic conditions. Among the most important aspects of being a primary care provider are quality of care, cost effectiveness, and patient satisfaction.

Coordinating care with other physicians

Coordination of care means carefully planning the activities and communicating patient preferences to all care providers. Proper coordination can improve the safety and quality of patient care. Information about patients' needs, preferences, and other details must be communicated to the right people at the right time. Primary care providers coordinate care with other physicians and other health professionals to ensure that patients receive safe and appropriate care. However, coordinating care can be challenging, and it can seem like too much work.

Research from Accenture shows that patients prefer their PCP to be the epicenter of care coordination. Almost three-quarters of respondents said that their primary care provider should be the epicenter of care coordination. This patient-centered approach extends beyond simply making referrals. Primary care providers are the first point of contact for patients with multiple medical conditions. Patients' experiences with a PCP may impact their care with other providers.

Lack of coordination of care between primary care physicians and other health providers can be dangerous. For example, patients may not get informed about the use of emergency departments unless they are referred to their primary care physicians. This lack of communication may lead to patients being prescribed medications that they are not able to tolerate. Primary care physicians may be able to advocate for less expensive care if they know more about their patients. A physician's knowledge of a patient's condition is crucial for the best care.

Integration of primary care and specialty care has become a critical component of a healthy health system. Increasing use of hospitalists and smaller practice consolidations may encourage PCPs to reduce their call responsibilities and maintain a more balanced lifestyle. However, increasing hospital ownership of primary care practices can also help physicians develop protocols for care coordination.

Building relationships with patients

Patients' first visits to their primary care providers often influence their attitude toward the healthcare provider, fostering the initial patient-provider relationship. A patient's initial judgment of a physician can affect a number of outcomes. Building relationships with patients is equally important in establishing trust and fostering positive health outcomes.

Patients should be involved in the decision-making process, which helps to establish trust between the patient and the physician. Building a good rapport requires compassion, empathy, and assertiveness. It also means that the patient feels heard, seen, and cared for. Finally, the relationship must be based on understanding and compassion. It can be difficult to overcome the barriers that prevent patient-provider relationships, but it is worth it in the long run.

Patient-provider relationships can benefit the patient in many ways. Oftentimes, patients feel more comfortable discussing sensitive issues and medical concerns with their primary care provider. Furthermore, patients are more likely to seek care from a physician who shares a common sense of values, including honesty. These factors can go a long way towards strengthening a patient-physician relationship. It can lead to better health outcomes.

Chapter 46 - What Is a Primary Caregiver (PCG)

Primary caregivers (PCGs) are the people most often in personal contact with the patient in their homes. They usually are with the patient for 4 to 8 hours or more at a given day for several days a week. PCGs typically are not employed by the home health agency. They may be outside caregivers from a third party agency, a family member helping out, or even a friend or neighbor doing a favor for the patient and their family.

PCGs are critical for home health agencies, however. Having a primary caregiver is actually a criteria for getting home health services. Typically the home health agency teaches the PCG certain skilled tasks if the patient is not capable of performing them, and the home health agency relies on the PCG in partnership with the patient to become more independent in the home.

PCGs significantly reduce the risk for rehospitalization for patients, similar to how seeing the PCP within 2 weeks reduces the risk of readmission to hospitals as well. Having the contact information of the PCG is a critical piece of data for nurse to gather so that the agency has a form of constant contact with the patient through phone, text, voicemail, or email.

Providing care for a loved one can be a tremendous burden. Thankfully, there are many options to relieve this burden. You can find help with mobility issues, providing emotional support, and lessening the burden of caregiving. Here are some tips for family primary care givers.

Responsibilities

Primary caregivers have responsibilities that range from basic assistance with daily activities to taking care of a patient's nutritional needs. Whether the patient lives with Alzheimer's or a different condition, the PCG can help ensure their daily needs are met. A primary caregiver may also take on the role of a household manager, tackling tasks such as laundry, grocery lists, and financial management. Caregivers often neglect their own health and well-being, and need assistance with daily activities. Fortunately, there are many services that can help caregivers manage this job.

Some primary caregiver responsibilities include assisting the care recipient with medication and errands. They may also assist with transportation and make sure the patient gets to doctor appointments. Additionally, they may help the care recipient get dressed and undress. Primary caregivers help their loved ones maintain their independence by helping them with routine activities, such as cleaning up after illness. They may even help the patient maintain a hobby or interest.

Primary caregivers must be aware of the fact that the task can be difficult, and they need to balance their own life with their duties. It is important to remember that the caregiving role is demanding and can lead to exhaustion. The primary caregiver's job may be so demanding that they must modify their schedule or even leave their job. They may have to give up their career and interrupt their education. However, there are resources available to support them and minimize their stress.

The duties of a primary caregiver vary greatly, and the type of care you are providing may be dependent on the condition of the person you are caring for. If you're caring for someone with Alzheimer's, the list will be a bit more extensive.

One of the most challenging roles a primary caregiver will have is caring for a parent who has become ill. The caregiver's stress levels can be extremely high, and the constant juggling of tasks may lead to caregiver burnout, which affects both mental and physical health. Additional financial burdens include a limited income and medical expenses. You may not be able to work full-time to meet these needs.

Bonding with patient

A positive emotional connection can be created between the caregiver and the patient. This connection creates a sense of trust between caregiver and patient, facilitating open communication between the two. The caregiver can discuss the care needs of the patient without causing resentment, allowing the caregiver to provide the best care possible. However, it is important to recognize that emotional connections are often difficult to establish. In order to create a positive emotional connection, caregivers should consider identifying what they need from their caregiver.

Family caregivers

As a family caregiver, you may be able to take advantage of various home health care programs to help you provide care for your loved one. First of all, you can check if your loved one is eligible for these programs. This way, you can get reimbursed for your services, such as with In Home Supportive Services (IHSS) benefits in California for those covered with MediCal.

Tax credits for family caregivers may be available. A bipartisan bill, the Credit for Caring Act, provides a tax credit to family caregivers for up to $2,000 in expenses related to caring for an elderly relative. This credit is available to caregivers who earn more than $7,500 a year and incur long-term care costs. This is typically when Medical Social Worker is useful to consult with to discuss these types of community resources that may be available to the patients and their families.

Family caregivers in home health services programs are also available to individuals who are not employed by a health care agency. These programs are run by the state's Department of Aging (DGA). Typically, these programs offer limited supplemental services to caregivers, such as prescription reminders, training, and counseling. Additionally, you'll have access to health care professionals, such as pharmacists and social workers, if needed.

While most family caregivers are responsible for providing assistance with IADLs (instrumental activities of daily living), the majority of family caregivers also assist their care recipients with personal hygiene tasks. In fact, 99 percent of the family caregivers provide assistance with meal preparation, transportation, and grocery shopping. Those ADLs are vital to a senior's health and well-being. But even though the number of family caregivers is small, it is still significant.

Unlike traditional home health care, a consumer-directed home-care program offers the advantage of allowing the care recipient to choose their caregiver. Under the program, you can choose between family members or friends who are eligible to work. The main difference is that spouses are not permitted to work as caregivers, and family caregivers can only be hired in rare cases, especially for elderly people with dementia or other serious conditions. If a family caregiver's financial situation is too tight, this program may be an option for you.

Chapter 47 - The Role of the Pharmacy

Dispensing

The pharmacy is an outside agency apart from the home health agency. The pharmacy is responsible for dispensing medications to patients after receiving orders from the patient's provider. For home health patients, they may receive their medications by mail. However, if patients do not have access to that service, their caregivers typically drive to the pharmacy and pick up their medications for them. Some pharmacies even set up reminders of patients to pick up their medications when it needs refilling.

Collaboration

Home health nurses, home health aides, and pharmacists can collaborate to improve patient outcomes by providing drug and treatment information. The importance of providing this information cannot be overstated. Patients often have questions and pharmacists can help by providing patient-friendly information. In the past, pharmacists have not collaborated well with nurses and home health aides. The lack of proximity and distance to hospitals and physicians can limit their collaboration. However, pharmacists and nurses can improve their working relationships by collaborating with other health care professionals.

Pharmacists have extensive training to provide basic health care services to patients. They can help patients manage diabetes by explaining how to use a glucometer and interpreting readings. They can also help patients find over-the-counter medications for common ailments. These services should be offered by pharmacists in home health. And pharmacists can also provide patients with information about the use of medications and the effects they may have on the body.

The pharmacists should be competent to perform the home health infusion. In addition to receiving proper training, pharmacists should take part in a competency assessment program and continue their education. The assessment of their knowledge, skills, and experience should be valid and documented. The pharmacists should provide accurate information to patients about their medication therapy. They should also be able to answer patients' questions and address their concerns in a concise and timely manner.

There are also various types of drug therapy and pharmacists play a pivotal role in managing and promoting cost-effective care. PBMs, hospitals, health plans, and accountable care organizations routinely utilize pharmacists to reduce costs and maximize patient outcomes. In addition, pharmacists can assist physicians and health care providers by assessing the effects of drug therapies, making recommendations, and recommending alternatives.

They should develop comprehensive services to address factors unique to home infusion

The development of comprehensive services is particularly important in a home infusion pharmacy because caregivers often lack adequate health care training and knowledge. It is critical for caregivers to be trained to administer medication and operate appropriate devices for their patients. Home health agencies are responsible for teaching caregivers and making sure caregivers perform the skilled medical tasks well. Moreover, many medications require aseptic compounding, in quantities sufficient to last for a week, and delivery under controlled conditions to ensure product potency and purity. Moreover, home infusion pharmacies should develop systems and policies that ensure quality and safety of care.

While home infusion pharmacies provide consultations by telephone, pharmacists should consider expanding their reach by developing a home visit program. Home visits should improve patient compliance and simplify complicated drug-related issues for patients. A pharmacist should be available 24 hours a day to answer questions. In addition, a home visit may be helpful to ease the transition from hospital to home. And pharmacists should take an active role in infection-control activities.

A pharmacy director should ensure the effective use of personnel and resources. The resources should be sufficient to protect patient confidentiality. The pharmacy director should ensure that staffing plans reflect factors such as weekend hours, flex time, and exempt or nonexempt status. The director should also consider other factors that affect pharmacy staffing, such as on-call pay and shift differentials. In addition, a pharmacist should ensure the confidentiality of patient information.

The pharmacist should document all clinical actions and recommendations in the home infusion patient's medical record. Moreover, pharmacists should consult other health professionals and document the consultations and outcomes in the patient's medical record. The pharmacy should develop a process for consistent documentation and reporting of services. Finally, pharmacists should ensure patient privacy at all times. There should be appropriate training for all employees working in a home infusion pharmacy.

SECTION 5 – Conclusion

Motivating Yourself, Motivating Your Patients, and Motivating Other Team Members

Chapter 48 - What is Motivation?

There are countless theories of human motivation, each of which sheds light on some aspect of it while ignoring others. While this diversity leads to a great deal of ambiguity, most of these theories share areas of overlap and disagreement. Regardless of their differences, each theory contributes a unique perspective, and their implications for practice differ significantly. Read on to learn about the many different theories of motivation. There is no single theory that best explains human behavior.

Motivation is a process

It is a dynamic force within the mind that causes people to act and move toward a goal. Several things can motivate people, such as rewards, punishments, or self-motivation. In most cases, motivation involves stimulating individuals to accomplish tasks. People are motivated by a variety of factors, including the fulfillment of needs and desires, the achievement of a desired goal, and the satisfaction of their own needs. In other cases, the motivation may occur in an individual only, and it may also come from other sources.

For example, high-motivated employees are more likely to remain in the organization and increase their earnings within it, and less likely to quit their jobs. A motivated employee will also be less likely to engage in absenteeism, poor work ethic, and labor unrest. Ultimately, this will improve the efficiency and effectiveness of the organization. High levels of motivation will also boost morale, which is a good thing for a business.

The process of motivation can be positive or negative, and can include a reward for good work or a demotion for non-performance. Positive motivation is a form of positive reinforcement, while negative motivation uses negative means to induce desired behaviors. As a result, the process of motivation is a dynamic one, and not all people respond to the same types of rewards and punishments. There is no "one size fits all" approach to motivation. Regardless of the motivational style, it should be ongoing.

Human beings have many basic needs. Physical needs include food, drink, and health. Psychological and social needs include safety, shelter, and old-age pension. They also have social needs, such as the desire for affection, and the desire to belong to society. The satisfaction of these basic needs allows people to achieve higher-order needs. If the primary needs are fulfilled, the motivational process will increase. This is a natural and cyclic process that occurs throughout our lives.

The importance of rewards is paramount to human motivation. In addition to the reward itself, expectancy also plays a vital role in determining how motivated a person is. As long as the rewards are valuable, people will feel motivated to work hard and complete the task. Depending on the outcome, this increase in motivation can make the difference between a productive employee and an unhappy one. However, it is important to recognize that the rewards and punishments of these actions are often not directly proportional.

It is important to note that sustaining motivation is difficult, even under the best circumstances. Often, the factors that inspire us differ from person to person. The key is to find something that works for you. Motivating yourself and your team will reward you in the end. When other people aren't pushing you, keep on pushing until the reward comes. Motivation is an ongoing process that takes time to change. If you're looking for a quick fix for an ailing motivation, the best way to get it is to change your attitude.

Chapter 49 - Motivating Yourself As a Nurse

You can find nursing jobs all over the country. Finding your own unique purpose in life will drive you through long hours and provide a solid reason to work hard. Hopefully that purpose is in home health as you read through this book. People who are truly motivated are those who enjoy their work and are excited to go to work each day. You can identify your own personal motivations by interviewing some of the most highly motivated people in your area.

Motivation levels and self-concept

A strong connection between self-esteem and professional self-concept and that a positive relationship between the two affects nursing students' motivation levels. Self-esteem, professional self-concept, and motivation levels all influence nursing students' overall performance. This study also found that nursing students with a higher self-esteem were more motivated than those with lower self-esteem. It also found that the higher self-esteem, the higher the motivation level, the better the nursing student performed in the clinical setting.

However, it is important to remember that high levels of knowledge and skill are necessary for successful nurses. Physicians value nurses with high levels of knowledge and accept them. Consequently, nurses with high levels of knowledge and skill are more confident at their work and have less anxiety through their work day. This in turn boosts clinical motivation and improves nurse's job satisfaction.

Need of competence in self-determination theory

Throughout our lives, we encounter many opportunities for mastery. This is why we develop different skills and strive to gain mastery in different areas. When we feel connected to others and that we have the skills to fulfill our needs, we are more likely to take action. Our environment also influences our level of competence. The environment of our family, friends, co-workers, health care professionals, and culture influence our psychological needs.

As a nurse, you may have to face challenges. You must be able to support patients' autonomy, while also ensuring their safety. This means respecting the rights of the patients and not controlling their behavior. As a nurse, you must understand and appreciate the value of autonomy in nursing practice. When working with patients, you must ensure that they are given the tools they need to make informed decisions.

It is important to understand the theoretical underpinnings of self-determination theory. Nurses need to consider intrinsic motivation when implementing behavioral change. This means understanding the motivation behind adherence to standards and medical instructions. Self-determination theory is an excellent way to understand trends in nursing. This theory also applies to self-regulatory behaviors, such as patient compliance with medical instructions. The need for autonomy motivates people to work on their own goals and achieve higher psychological wellbeing.

Need of competence in self-determination theory in nursing is important for the future of a nursing career. It is important for a nurse to be competent in all areas of nursing and to have sufficient knowledge to carry out a given task. In addition, self-determination theory helps people become more autonomous by helping them develop the skills they need for a career. If you have this skill set, then you are well on your way to achieving your goals.

Fueling your body with healthy foods to stay motivated

To stay physically fit, nurses must eat the right foods. Ideally, they should eat several small meals a day, but they can also pack in snacks. Nurses should limit the amount of fast food they eat, and aim to limit their intake of processed and sugary food. For nutrition tips, visit Daily Nurse, which offers eating hacks for busy nurses.

Caring for other people can wear on the mind and body. When you work long hours, you may be tempted to reach for sugary foods in the break room or grab something from the vending machine. You may also be tempted to eat unhealthy food from co-workers. The pressure of a 12-hour shift can leave you little time to prepare a healthy meal. Furthermore, other commitments outside of work can reduce the amount of time you have to prepare a nutritious meal.

Taking breaks

Taking breaks is an effective way to boost your productivity. The main goal of taking breaks is to stop focusing and recharge. The benefits of these short breaks are many. By doing so, you can return to your work refreshed and ready to perform at your best. In addition to providing you with time to recharge, taking breaks is also beneficial for your health. Here are some tips to make the most of your breaks at work.

Take regular breaks. Research shows that taking breaks has several benefits, including increased productivity. It has been shown that human brains are not wired to focus for eight hours without any break, and the average workday has only three hours of productive time. Breaking from your work can reduce mental fatigue and help you stay focused. In addition to increasing your productivity, taking breaks will make you a happier and more productive worker. Take a break from your work when you need it!

Take short breaks. Short breaks provide the PFC with a brief respite and revitalize. Short breaks help employees remain focused, improve motivation, and boost their creativity. Also, walking around is great for both physical and mental health. Even a few minutes of walking around is beneficial. By taking regular breaks, you will find that you feel refreshed and ready to tackle any task you have. And you'll be glad you did.

Schedule your breaks. If your day is long, a break will help you regain your energy and get back to work with increased productivity. If you're distracted, it can prevent you from achieving your goals. Instead of allowing distractions to ruin your focus, you should plan a break for yourself to rejuvenate. Breaks will give you time to think about your work and come up with solutions to problems.

Having an accountability partner or study group

The benefits of an accountability partner are obvious, but there are several other benefits, too. An accountability partner helps you set short-term goals and reminds you of the deadlines. It also helps you stay grounded and avoid over-optimism. Accountability partners are also good for reflection. They will make sure you stay focused on the present. A mentor will guide you along your path to nursing success, not only provide advice, but also provide valuable information that will improve your performance.

Another benefit of having an accountability partner is that it can help you make improvements in your work. Many nurses work in teams, and it is important to make sure that everyone is happy with the job. If you are not comfortable offering feedback, find someone who is. You can then share your knowledge with them. Sharing knowledge helps your team improve, and it strengthens bonds among nurses. If possible, offer to mentor a teammate, too. This will help you develop better professional relationships and help you become more effective in your role.

An accountability partner can help you stay focused on your goals. A good accountability partner can be a coworker, friend, or family member. It is important to set up a system for check-ins and keep each other motivated. This can also be an excellent source of motivation for you. When you have someone to hold you accountable, you will be more likely to complete tasks and work on your goals.

Finding a distinctive purpose at work

Many people struggle with burnout, but finding a distinct purpose at work is essential for recapturing enthusiasm and joy. Knowing why you're doing what you do makes the work much easier. Nursing jobs are available across the U.S., so you're likely to find one near you. There are several benefits of finding a purpose at work, such as a satisfying career, helping others, or even changing people's lives.

A sense of purpose is vital for living a rewarding healthcare career. A hospital or clinic or home health agency is much more successful when its staff members are energized and engaged. Their purpose is built into their lives and helps them make a difference. In addition, purposeful people are happier, more productive, and less likely to burn out. Leaders who support their team members in finding their purpose are likely to have happier employees.

Chapter 50 - Strategies For Motivating Your Patients

This chapter discusses strategies for motivating your patients. These include building rapport, using mirror neurons, and setting realistic goals. By following these tips, you can make your patients happier and more likely to comply with your orders. Use these methods to motivate your patients and keep them motivated and engaged throughout their recovery. They will thank you! Using motivational interviewing techniques and mirror neurons to engage your patients is an effective way to help them achieve their goals.

Motivational interviewing

The research to validate the effectiveness of Motivational Interviewing for patients focuses on two dimensions of change: confidence and self-efficacy. The former is a person's belief that they are capable of changing their behavior. The latter is the belief that the person can achieve their goals. In general, motivational interviewing helps patients increase their confidence and self-efficacy. Patients can learn to express their own goals and why they need to make the change.

A recent meta-analysis of studies found that treatment outcomes after a brief motivational interview were statistically significant. Three of the studies examined different variables, including willingness to engage in treatment for substance use, referral to a specialist, and written summaries. Overall, these studies indicated a positive effect on patients' attitudes and behavior. However, it is still unclear whether this type of intervention will increase patient commitment and success with change.

While addressing the patient's reluctance to change, clinicians must consider the setting in which the patient lives. For example, a patient may attend an eating disorder clinic and eventually be admitted to a specialized hospital. The clinician should emphasize the patient's values and identify obstacles that prevent them from achieving their goals. In this way, a patient-centered approach can be successful. The clinician should be empathic to address patients' ambivalence toward change and the fact that the change they seek is usually part of a better daily lifestyle.

Building rapport

Research shows that building rapport with patients is crucial for the healing process. According to a 2014 study published in PLOS Medicine, patients with a positive relationship with their healthcare providers provide better clinical information and are more likely to follow up. Besides, rapport can help reduce stress. Moreover, patients with a positive relationship with their healthcare providers are more likely to provide accurate and honest information. To create a positive rapport with patients, follow up with them regularly and listen to their concerns.

During difficult conversations, you should use measured voice and mirror your patient. If possible, maintain a friendly demeanor and use the right language. Make sure to communicate any changes in your patient's ability to complete tasks and keep your word. When possible, practice all of these techniques. Pick ones that feel natural to you and practice them. After all, you are building rapport with your patients!

Rapport is commonly used in healthcare and is assumed to be a fundamental part of professional-patient relationships. While rapport is a general term, specific studies have attempted to define it more specifically in the health field. Many studies have also tried to define other complex terms used in healthcare such as person-centered care and resilience. But there is no consensus about its definition. For the purposes of this article, rapport has been defined as "a sense of trust and a shared understanding between a health care professional and a patient."

Rapport is an important part of any healthcare relationship and should be cultivated in the early stages of patient-care encounters. Good rapport leads to positive patient outcomes, better adherence to treatments, and improved patient satisfaction. As a result, it is important to train healthcare professionals in interpersonal communication and to incorporate it into their daily practice. This article has been structured to analyze literature on these two concepts. It will be discussed further in future research on these topics.

Using mirror neurons

Mirror neurons are brain regions involved in the imitation of simple movements and learning complex skills. They also play a role in perception, communication, and theory of mind. Moreover, mirror neurons help us share our feelings and sensations. This understanding is beneficial for both patients and caregivers. Here are some tips on how to motivate your patients by using mirror neurons.

The connection between mirrored neuronal activity and empathy is an obvious advantage. When we see the emotions of others, we interpret them the same way. Our mirror neurons help us understand how others feel. The same emotion can cause different reactions from different people, which helps us understand how to respond to those emotions. Besides, mirror neurons are also helpful in motivational and empathy counseling. They can help your patients learn to interact better in social settings, even if they are struggling with mental health issues.

Research on mirror neurons began in the 1990s when scientists studied nonhuman primates. They found that when humans watched another primate grab an object, a certain part of their brain fired. These signals were similar to the actual action potentials. The results of this study suggest that mirror neurons can help motivate patients. This research has several benefits, and will continue to inspire more research in the field. So, don't hesitate to use mirror neurons in your daily clinical practice.

A recent study has revealed the relationship between human motor and speech. Mirror neurons can help patients improve their motor skills by recognizing how they are responding to other people. The authors of this paper explain how mirror neurons are involved in motor and language processing. Their findings have implications for the treatment of a wide range of neurological disorders. They also provide arguments for and against the role of mirror neurons in speech perception. There is a strong connection between verbal speech and gesture-based language.

Setting realistic goals

To motivate patients to make positive changes in their life, set meaningful goals for them. Each patient is unique in their personality, life circumstances, and hopes for the future. Setting goals that are meaningful to your patient's life is a collaborative effort that taps into the intrinsic drive that motivates them to change. The key is to set goals that your patients can actually achieve. To help them reach their goals, consider the following tips.

Choose an activity that patients can enjoy. If they hate physical activity, they are unlikely to stay consistent and may give up altogether. A patient can ask a colleague to join a walking club, or join a mall walking group. Parents can engage in physical activities with their children. By setting an example for them to follow, they can model a healthy lifestyle for their children. If you want to motivate your patients to be active, set goals that are achievable but stretchable.

Set meaningful goals for your patients. Patients should identify which behaviors they want to change and which ones they enjoy. It may also help to include emotional goals. If your patients have emotional problems, they might need to address them before setting goals. Likewise, patients should define why they want to change. If you help them create meaningful goals, they will feel motivated and be more likely to meet them. If they set goals that are not meaningful, they will be less likely to achieve them.

Write down your goals. Creating a written goal can help you remember the details of it. It will also help you stay motivated and focused. Setting goals is also an excellent way to boost your self-esteem. You can use the SMART method to set goals, a structured framework that includes letters and numbers related to the desired outcome. This framework will help you set realistic goals that are both attainable and achievable.

Chapter 51 - How to Motivate Your Coworkers

Here are some ways to motivate them and increase their commitment to the team. As a leader, you should be patient, empathize with their struggles, offer solutions, and reward hard work. Working with uncommitted coworkers can be frustrating. Here are some ways to motivate your coworkers so that you can get the best results possible.

Working together as a team

Motivating coworkers by working together as one team is a proven way to boost morale. This type of collaborative effort builds bonds between team members and creates a sense of belonging among them. Teamwork also requires people to pitch in and help one another. The team can change direction as required, giving flexibility and adaptability to its circumstances. If it's done right, it can even motivate the most resistant employees.

A Stanford faculty member, Gregory Walton, co-authored a paper in the Journal of Experimental Psychology that found that "cues to work as a team" increased intrinsic motivation in participants. In other words, people want to do work that's intrinsically rewarding. But, what is intrinsic motivation? In psychology, motivation comes from within and is derived from personal values and goals. If it comes from within, people tend to sustain their motivation over time. By working together as a team, the team can make a difference and be a positive force for a company.

To motivate coworkers to work as a team, create challenges for the team. Make the team members take on a challenge together, such as saving money or improving service. Physical challenges also help in team bonding. Provide training and advancement opportunities for team members so they can learn to work well together. Make sure everyone on the team is working together fairly, regardless of the role they play. This way, everyone has an opportunity to contribute to the team's success.

Work in teams can help motivate individuals by fostering a sense of friendship and loyalty. Teamwork creates a positive work environment and can allow employees to work harder without feeling lonely. Moreover, it prevents individual problems from affecting the team's productivity. This is a highly valuable asset in the workplace. It helps the employees to get along with each other and accomplish tasks faster. There are fewer problems and stress when working in teams.

Being a compassionate listener

Compassionate listening is essential in any work environment. It ensures a healthy flow of communication and increases employee retention. Research shows that employees who receive empathy from coworkers are more likely to stay with an organization and work efficiently. By being compassionate, you will help employees feel more valued and appreciated.

Empathy is a vital part of being a good leader, employee, and colleague. Empathy is a trait that every employer looks for when hiring new employees. Natural leaders are incredibly motivating and excellent collaborators. They put the well-being of the team before their own goals and success. Fortunately, you can train yourself to be compassionate and empathic, even if you don't have an MBA. It can be learned through training and exposure, so you can develop your awareness of other people's lives, values, and motivations.

Compassionate leadership is a practice that blurs the line between self and others, fostering a sense of belonging and trust. When you show compassion to others, you create an environment in which diverse people can be creative, enthusiastic, and productive. A compassionate leader never fails to ask questions, solicit feedback, and communicate effectively with his or her coworkers. And because compassion is an integral component of service, it makes leaders feel good about themselves.

Being a compassionate leader requires empathy and compassion. Compassionate leaders acknowledge the challenges of others, enabling them to thrive in their work. They are aware of their own limitations and strengths, and are open to new approaches and strategies. By empathizing with other people, compassionate leaders are able to build a culture of understanding and compassion within their organization. So, be compassionate while motivating your coworkers!

Offering solutions

The first step in motivating your coworkers is to be approachable and listen to their concerns. It is essential to constantly communicate with your employees, since you should know their grievances and expectations. If you take the time to hear them out, you'll build a positive atmosphere and increase morale. Additionally, it's important to show your coworkers that you believe in them and their abilities. This will boost their confidence and productivity, so don't forget to show them that they are valued.

Another effective way to motivate your coworkers is by setting a good example. Be a sounding board for their concerns. Oftentimes, coworkers feel unappreciated and uninspired by their work. By acting as a sounding board for their ideas, you'll encourage them to do the same. In addition, a supportive colleague will serve as an ally, and the positive environment will inspire them to work harder.

Rewarding hard work

Rewarding hard work as a motivational tool can be incredibly effective. Employees who feel appreciated and recognized are more likely to stay at a company and show more loyalty. Rewarding employees with a high-quality reward shows that you recognize their efforts and appreciate them. Employees feel more engaged and motivated to work hard for you. It's important that you never underestimate the power of recognition.

Recognizing hard work and mentioning it in meetings can be an effective way to motivate employees. Praise can be given when deliverables are completed on time or work is completed ahead of schedule. High-performing employees may feel valued and rewarded when they receive praise or mention that they contributed to the company's success. By offering praises and rewards in front of their coworkers, they will feel recognized and appreciated. Rewarding employees during impromptu meetings can make them feel valued and appreciated.

Employees want to feel appreciated for their efforts. A well-deserved reward will keep them motivated and happy. The best way to do this is to recognize their contributions. Rewarding your coworkers for hard work and completing projects is one of the best ways to motivate them. Employees want to feel recognized for their efforts, but this recognition doesn't have to involve monetary or prize money. Companies like Deloitte, for example, use software to reward their workers by allowing them to appear on leadership boards and earn badges. Employees who consistently receive recognition and feedback will continue to work hard.

When employees are tired or overwhelmed, they won't produce the best work. Rewarding hard work in this way creates a healthy competition between coworkers. Ultimately, rewards are essential for high-quality work. But don't forget to consider the mental, emotional, and physical health of your employees. By measuring motivation, you'll be able to create a successful incentive program.

Transparency in the workplace

If you want to inspire your employees, you should practice transparency. Be honest about your plans and expectations, and keep everyone updated. Make sure that you have open-door policies and conduct regular meetings to communicate what's expected from your team. If you're not transparent about certain things, this can cause animosity and a lack of respect for you. Embrace transparency in your own life as well as your business.

Openness about salaries is a good way to encourage open communication and encourage open discussions. While salary discussions are typically taboo in many cultures, the openness and communication of salary can lead to a more positive working environment. It also helps to eliminate discrimination and foster a sense of togetherness and recognition of similar accomplishments. Transparency will improve your productivity and employee engagement, which will result in greater happiness and creative thinking.

One key to increasing employee engagement is creating an environment where employees are transparent about company goals and practices. Transparency opens up new lines of conversation, and creates opportunities to tap into hidden resources. MIT senior lecturer Otto Scharmer explains that 'why' is critical, and sharing goals and objectives openly is an important way to create a culture of trust. It also helps employees align their work with higher-level goals.

Creating an environment where people are openly and honestly communicating will help the company grow. Transparency builds trust, which increases employee productivity. Ultimately, this can help you improve customer service and boost revenue. With better transparency, you'll have a happier team, which results in better productivity, higher profits, and excellent customer-client relations. There's no reason you shouldn't follow the example of transparency if you want to motivate your employees.

Chapter 52 - Philosophy of Nursing Ideals and Beliefs

The philosophy of nursing is very personal to each and every nurse. There is no right or wrong answer to it, but your philosophy of nursing is what you make of it and it is unique to you. It combines values, ideals, and beliefs to develop a theoretical framework for professional practice.

Non-nursing philosophers also contribute to the philosophy of nursing, addressing key concepts in the practice of nursing. For example, Jacques Maritain explored the relationship between reason and intuition, and Mary Clark elaborated the metaphysical assumptions about human persons. Alas MacIntyre considered contemporary ethical thinking, while Edith Stein proposed a phenomenological understanding of empathy and a theory of values. And Mette Lebech explored the notion of human dignity.

Values

A nurse's personal philosophy of nursing is a reflection of their individual values. This statement serves as a guide to their daily work, and it provides focus and motivation to fulfill their responsibilities. The philosophy also reflects the individual's willingness to change and adapt. Here are a few tips to help you develop your own personal nursing philosophy:

Ethical principles define the behavior of nurses, and they include respect and dignity of individuals. Social justice also involves ensuring equal access to health care services for everyone, regardless of race, gender, or culture. Finally, it calls for ethical decision-making. Nursing students should strive to develop appropriate skills and acquire knowledge necessary for their career. These principles should guide their professional practice, and nursing educators should adopt them according to local, national, and religious conditions.

Personal and professional values guide the behavior and attitude of a nurse. Personal values are formed by cultural influences and personal needs, while professional values influence nursing practices and responsibilities. A nurse's personal philosophy will guide her decisions and actions to achieve the desired patient outcome. Nursing values will also guide her teaching and research. An appropriate nursing philosophy will guide her to provide compassionate care, but will also promote health and healing for those she serves. If nursing philosophy is important to you, be sure to make time for your personal reflection on the subject.

As a nurse, you may also consider how you relate to your role and what drives you. For example, you may value collaborating with other healthcare professionals in their mission. Or, you may enjoy collaborating with patients to improve their health. If this is true, incorporating your personal connection to your role into your nursing philosophy will motivate you and guide you throughout your career. And in a hospital, nursing values can include making a difference in the lives of patients.

Ideals

Nursing philosophy is an important part of a nurse's practice. The values derived from nursing philosophy guide the work of nurses. They help nurses remain committed and focused on the daily tasks, while also inspiring persistence. They guide nurses in navigating difficult decisions and help them evaluate the responsibilities they have. There are many ideals of nursing philosophy to choose from. Each philosophy has its advantages and disadvantages, but they all have a common purpose: to improve the lives of patients.

The character of a nurse also plays an important role in nursing philosophy. Nurses should respect the dignity of patients, and act without discrimination. They should not make a distinction based on race, religion, financial status, or physical disability. They must be compassionate, and be able to listen to the patients' needs. Nursing philosophy emphasizes the importance of being compassionate, attentive, and understanding. The character of a nurse is an essential element of the work of a nurse.

An individual's ideals of nursing philosophy should be unique. Florence Nightingale, for instance, believed that nursing was a spiritual calling. She believed that each patient had a spiritual dimension. Therefore, nurses were called to serve others and help them in their spiritual distress. Any nurse can create a philosophy of nursing based on their own beliefs and theories, but it's important to remember that the statements must be true to who they are.

Beliefs

Beliefs in nursing philosophy are a personal statement of how you view the world and the work you do. Nursing philosophy helps nurses make decisions and stay motivated by providing a higher purpose. By identifying your own personal philosophy, you can make a difference in your nursing career and stand out from other candidates in a highly competitive industry.

As a nurse, you must take the uniqueness of every individual into account. You must work to ensure that each person has access to high-quality care, reduce health disparities, and reach out to vulnerable groups. Ultimately, nursing is about helping people. It is a privilege to help others. Nursing philosophy emphasizes these ideals. Beliefs about human dignity are important to consider when implementing nursing practices.

Personal values: Having a personal nursing philosophy helps nurses define their core values. These values determine their work and behaviors. Having a philosophy allows nurses to stay connected to their purpose and mission. Personal nursing philosophy allows them to understand the meaning of their work and the impact it has on their patients and the community. It can also inspire nurses to work for a purpose beyond their career. It can even lead to a successful career.

Steps to writing a personal philosophy of nursing

Your personal philosophy of nursing statement should be short and concise. It should explain your personal reasons for becoming a nurse, which may be theoretical or emotional. You should define nursing in terms of its importance to society and the underprivileged. It should also describe what roles you play in the nursing profession and why you feel that role is important. In writing your philosophy, you need to keep in mind your own values and beliefs.

When you're writing your personal philosophy of nursing, remember that your beliefs and values are at the heart of your personal and professional life. They help you make decisions, practice nursing skills, and lead a life of service. You might be aware of your own personal beliefs, or you may be able to uncover them through a reflective exercise. In either case, your philosophy of nursing is your unique combination of beliefs, values, skills, and traits that define your unique character and approach to the profession.

A personal philosophy of nursing should give the reader a sense of purpose and help them define their own professional values. It helps them focus on their day-to-day tasks, and helps them measure the difficulties of difficult decisions. A personal philosophy of nursing is a valuable tool for nurses. It can make a difference in their career. It may even inspire future employees to pursue a nursing career.

Chapter 53 - The Importance of Self Care for Nurses

The importance of self care for nurses is often underestimated or ignored by professional nurses. Taking breaks and using your own time are two key ways to prioritize self care. Regardless of your role, you deserve time to relax and rejuvenate. You owe it to yourself to give yourself the attention you deserve.

Misinterpretation of self-care by professional nurses

The concept of self-care is an important one. It involves making decisions on one's own behalf to improve one's health and wellbeing. Self-care practices also involve social interaction, learning, and developing knowledge and skills. In short, self-care improves physical, mental, emotional, and spiritual health. In fact, self-care practices can also prevent diseases. By engaging in self-care activities, nurses can increase their sense of autonomy, which is essential to their job.

However, the concept of self-care has been largely ignored by professional nurses. The Nurses Pledge of Service, which states that patient care is the first priority, has contributed to confusion in the nursing community. In many cases, nursing professionals misunderstand self-care as selfish behavior and consider it to be a sign of selfishness. This misinterpretation can lead to stress, depression, and feelings of worthlessness and helplessness.

Common barriers to self-care for nurses

Although nurses are integral to the fight against lifestyle-related diseases, many of them do not engage in healthy self-care practices. To identify barriers to self-care and promote health, we used qualitative content analysis to examine nurses' perceptions of facilitators and barriers to health-promoting behavior. Findings from this study revealed seven themes: lack of time and resources, "unhealthy" food, culture, fatigue, external commitments, and positive and negative role models.

Addressing these barriers requires a combination of interpersonal, intrapersonal, and institutional change.

While nurses are aware of the importance of self-care, implementing it is not always easy. Nurses face many challenges in developing and maintaining healthy habits, including conflicting work and home responsibilities, time, and money. However, self-care is crucial for nurses' wellbeing. In fact, 87 percent of nurses report that they could take better care of themselves if they had more time, although they report spending only four hours a day on physical activity, two hours per day watching television, and 280 minutes at a desk.

Setting limits and boundaries to prioritize self-care for nurses

The role of nursing is demanding and stressful, but there are ways to relieve some of the stress from this occupation. A recent study found that more than 80 percent of nurses reported varying degrees of mental and physical effects from the COVID-19 pandemic. Nursing also relies on compassion and empathy, two skills that are often compromised if nurses are stressed. A nurse who is depleted of these skills may not be able to provide the necessary care for patients.

Self-care for nurses is particularly important in a profession that requires close attention to patients and their needs. Nursing is one of the most stressful professions, and a nurse may not have enough time to prioritize her own needs. However, intentional self-care can keep a nurse physically, mentally, and spiritually healthy. Taking time to focus on your own health is a critical skill that every nurse must master.

Self-care for nurses doesn't have to be a big project. Start small and start with things you enjoy doing. Start small, and build up from there. Many nurses feel like they don't have time for self-care. The results of ignoring your own needs are negative. Rather than feeling guilty about it, try taking advantage of others and setting aside time to do what you love.

In order to develop effective interventions for nurse self-care, research should interview professional nurses and focus on how these models have helped them. Ultimately, the goal of such research is to help nurses prioritize their self-care. In addition to conducting interviews with nurses, nursing programs should also focus on how effective the model is in promoting health. If nurses are interested in developing a self-care education program, they can sign up for an online course or sign up for a self-care workshop.

Taking breaks to prioritize self-care for nurses

Self-care for nurses is crucial to their overall health, and nursing is no exception. Self-care for nurses means setting boundaries and guarding your productivity. It can be hard to say no to patients or to other tasks, but self-care can go a long way in reducing stress and anxiety. Nursing is a demanding, unpredictable profession, and it takes its toll on a nurse's mind and body. Nurses who practice self-care are more effective caregivers, and patients benefit from it.

Another way to prioritize self-care for nurses is to take intentional pauses. Listening to podcasts, taking a short walk after paying bills, or writing a journal can all help you take care of yourself. These intentional pauses help nurses avoid burnout and boost their mood and memory. In addition, fresh air can make you feel more alert and energized when you return to work. Taking breaks can help a nurse feel better about themselves and their ability to give quality care to others.

Taking breaks to prioritize self-care for nursing is essential for nurses' well-being. Since nurses work in high-stress environments, it's vital for them to learn how these stressful environments impact their physical and mental health. If needed, nurses can also turn to counseling and therapists for advice. There are a number of services near them, and their employers should offer their employees a counseling service if they need it.

Taking breaks to prioritize self-care for nursing is important for nurses' health. Self-care doesn't make you selfish, but it is important for their overall wellbeing. Nurses who prioritize self-care are better equipped to handle their daily challenges. For example, 70% of nurses say that their patients' health is their highest priority. However, nurses cannot give the best care when their cups are empty. Instead, they must make time to do things they enjoy.

Chapter 54 - Being a Lifelong Learner As a Nurse

Embracing a growth mindset is essential to being a lifelong learner in your career. It also means being self-motivated and willing to learn from others. Follow these tips and you'll be well on your way to being a lifelong learner as a nurse!

Embrace a growth mindset

Embrace a growth mindset as if it was a project: view your tasks as a journey and treat each setback as an opportunity to learn something new. If you are working towards a goal, break it down into milestones and try again. The more you practice the growth mindset, the easier it will be to adapt and overcome any obstacles that you may encounter along the way. Embracing a growth mindset as a nurse can make the difference between success and failure.

Growth mindset individuals are those who strive to improve their skills and competence over time. They strive for challenges, seek difficulty, learn from mistakes, persist for long periods, and lament when they get low grades. They also embrace difficult assignments, learn from others, and collaborate with colleagues. This mindset helps individuals achieve their career goals. If you are a nurse, embrace it today! It will lead to greater success and happiness.

The power of a growth mindset is enormous. People who adopt this mindset have a positive attitude and believe that they are capable of developing their skills and knowledge. This mindset is often associated with optimism, and is a strong foundation for success. While it may sound abstract, it can have enormous benefits for your career. If you're unsure about your skills, try embracing a growth mindset and embrace challenges as opportunities to learn.

Growth mindset individuals view mistakes as stepping stones to success. They see failure as an opportunity to learn from mistakes, and seek out mentors who can help them improve. They are willing to work hard, take risks, and seek out challenging situations. In short, they embrace challenges as learning experiences. This will lead to greater satisfaction, and help you achieve your career goals faster. It also gives you a competitive edge over others.

Be self-motivated

One way to stay motivated while working as a nurse is to become a lifelong learner. According to a report published by the Institute of Medicine and the Robert Wood Johnson Foundation, nursing education should focus on self-directed learning. Nurses should strive to improve their practice and stay current on new technologies. However, many nurses do not have the time or resources to pursue continuing education. To increase your personal knowledge, you can start a new course, join a nursing association, or take a class.

Nurse educators should encourage students to become self-motivated. Increasingly, nurse education is adopting student-centered approaches. The new courses must accommodate these approaches and foster student motivation. This type of learning is different than traditional classroom settings. In a student-centered approach, a nurse is required to interact more with her classmates, but she doesn't necessarily have to be present in the classroom.

Being a lifelong learner requires a self-motivated mindset and the ability to set goals and stick to them. Setting aside a consistent amount of time each week for learning is helpful and can lead to new certifications and further education. It can also be rewarding to increase your knowledge by taking on new tasks. The possibilities are endless. When you are motivated to learn, you will never stop.

Nursing students who have high levels of self-motivation tendencies had high levels of achievement-focused motivation. Achievement-focused motivation was associated with higher lifelong learning tendencies in nursing students. This tendency was associated with the student's choice of profession. The findings suggest that nursing students should pursue lifelong learning to increase their career satisfaction. They should also develop strategies to encourage students to pursue lifelong learning.

Be open to new information

As nurses become more valued decision-makers in health care teams, it is essential that they are open to new information. Nurses are often encouraged to use evidence-based practices, but the process of evidence-based practice is often viewed as passive rather than active. In the process of implementing research, nurses tend to overlook other sources of information. Research and colleagues are also valuable sources of information. Nursing professionals can also use their own experience and perspective to inform their work.

Be willing to learn from others

One of the most important characteristics of a good nurse is the ability to think critically. Critical thinking is an important skill to have because it helps nurses put knowledge into practice, especially when it comes to high-stress situations. Critical thinking is also crucial in applying clinical guidelines to patient care. Good nurses have a high critical thinking ability, and it is easy to notice when they demonstrate this quality. This skill can be cultivated over time, but it may be more natural to some nurses than others.

In a rapidly changing healthcare environment, nurses must be continually learning and gaining knowledge. Learning is essential for enhancing professional development, job satisfaction, and continuous improvement of patient care. Nurses have been shown to view themselves as lifelong learners and actively seek socially-oriented learning activities, especially when undergoing uncertain situations or trying to improve their technical nursing skills. In addition, nurses seek confirmation of their knowledge from co-workers, who may be able to provide a different perspective and experience.

Get online

Become a lifelong learner in nursing by pursuing your BSN. The nursing profession has gained increasing importance with the emergence of lifelong learning. Nurses are expected to use evidence-based practices, yet only half of nursing practice is supported by research. In addition to continuing to develop their skills, lifelong learners also engage in networks of resources that support their continuing education. New information improves the quality of healthcare systems and patient outcomes.

To promote the importance of lifelong learning, nursing organizations are promoting lifelong learning. Certification provides concrete proof of learning, making it a noteworthy way to demonstrate one's ongoing education. However, while nursing organizations and associations are promoting lifelong learning, the responsibility for nurse continuing education lies with individual registered nurses.

Online programs are an excellent option for completing continuing education requirements. Online learning is convenient and effective for busy professionals, nursing schools, and industry associations. This digital format accommodates a variety of technologies and allows nurses to complete the learning objectives and activities at their own pace. It also eliminates commute costs and streamlines subject matter updates. Moreover, with online learning, there is no physical requirement to attend an on-campus training. So, you can become an effective and valuable member of your industry! Be a lifelong learner nurse today!

Appendix A - Download the SOC Checklist Here

OASISNinja.com

To download either of the Comprehensive SOC checklist or Simple SOC Oasis checklist seen here, go to
OasisNinja.com/checklist

Recommended Further Reading

Check out more books by the author at
<u>OASISNinja.com</u>

Leave a Review!

I would really appreciate it if you would leave a review on Amazon after your purchase and let me know what you think, whether good or bad. It will go a long way in improving the quality of this book and books in the future. Thank you!

Appendix B - Selected References

Bowles, D. (2015). Gerontology Nursing Case Studies: 100+ Narratives for Learning 2nd Edition. Springer Publishing Company.

Barry, C. (2015). Nursing Case Studies in Caring: Across the Practice Spectrum 1st Edition. Springer Publishing Company.

Berkowitz, A. (2021). Clinical Pathophysiology Made Ridiculously Simple Ed 2. MedMaster Inc.

Billings, D, & Halstead, J. (2016). Teaching in Nursing: A Guide for Faculty. Elsevier.

Carby, A. (2013). The Nurse's Guide To Home Health Care: A handbook for nurses who are ready for positive change. CreateSpace Independent Publishing Platform.

CMS. (2022). Medicare Program - General Information. U.S. Centers for Medicare & Medicaid Services.

Dunphy, L., et al. (2015). Primary Care: Art and Science of Advanced Practice Nursing 4th Edition. F.A. Davis Company.

Edelman, C, et al. (2014). Health Promotion Throughout the Life Span. Elsevier Mosby.

Empyema, L. (2020). Nursing Narrative Note Examples to Save Your License: Charting and Documentation Suggestions for RNs & LPNs Who Have to Describe the Indescribable in a Medical Record. Independently Published.

Empyema, L. (2021). SOAP Note Examples & Documentation Tips: For Nurse Practitioners in Primary Care. Independently Published.

Gaberson, K, et al. (2014). Clinical Teaching Strategies in Nursing. Springer.

Gelety, K. (2010). Nursing Notes the Easy Way: 100+ Common Nursing Documentation and Communication Templates. Nursingthings.

Gonzalo, A. (2021). Dorothea Orem: Self-Care Deficit Theory. Nurselabs.

Hartweg, D. (1991). Dorothea Orem: Self-Care Deficit Theory (Notes on Nursing Theories) [Book]. SAGE Publications, Inc.

Haws, J. (2015). Nursing Case Studies: 15 Med Surg Case Studies with Rationales. NRSNG.com | NursingStudentBooks.com.

Hitchings, A. (2014). The Top 100 Drugs: Clinical Pharmacology and Practical Prescribing 1st Edition. Churchill Livingstone.

Irshad Ali, B. (2018). Application of Orem Self Care Decit Theory on Psychiatric Patient. Annals of Nursing and Practice.

Kolcaba, K. (2018). Kolcaba's Comfort Theory. Nursology.net.

Kolcaba, K. (2002). Comfort Theory and Practice: A Vision for Holistic Health Care and Research. Springer Publishing Company.

Krulish, L & Bernier, M. (2022) Blueprint for OASIS Accuracy: Data Collection Workshop. OASIS Answers, Inc.

Lippincot Williams & Wilkins. (2016). Health Assessment Made Incredibly Visual (Incredibly Easy! Series®) Third Edition. LWW.

Marelli, T. (2018). Handbook of Home Health Standards, Marrelli red book, staff education, OASIS, care planning, successful career in home health Spiral-bound. Marrelli and Associates, Inc.

Maldonado, D. (2018). SOAP for Family Medicine 2nd Edition. LWW.

MedBridge. (n.d.). Retrieved from https://www.medbridgeeducation.com/

Neal-Boylan, L. (2011). Clinical Case Studies in Home Health Care 1st Edition. Wiley-Blackwell.

Papadakis, M., et al. (2022). CURRENT Medical Diagnosis and Treatment 2023 62nd Edition. McGraw Hill.

Perry, A & Potter, P. (2018). Mosby's Pocket Guide to Nursing Skills & Procedures (Nursing Pocket Guides) 9th Edition. Mosby.

Wijesinghe, S. (2020). 101 Primary Care Case Studies: A Workbook for Clinical and Bedside Skills 1st Edition. Springer Publishing Company.

Lawson, S. (2021). House Calls 101: The Complete Clinician's Guide To In-Home Health Care, Telemedicine Services, and Long-Distance Treatment For a Post-Pandemic World (Housecalls 101 Book 2). A DrNurse Publishing House.

Marrelli, T. (2016). Home Care Nursing: Surviving In An Ever-changing Care Environment. Sigma Theta Tau International.

Neal-Noylan, L. (2011). Clinical Case Studies in Home Health Care. John Wiley & Sons, Inc.

Maag, J. (2015). How to Start a Home Health Care Agency. Jeffie Magg (self published).

Harris, M. (2015). Handbook of Home Health Care Administration 6th Edition. Jones & Bartlett Learning.

McCance, K. & Huether, S. (2014). Pathophysiology: The Biologic Basis for Disease in Adults and Children. Mosby.

Mason, D. (2016). Policy & Politics in Nursing and Health Care, Seventh Edition. Elsevier Inc.

McEwen, M. (2019). Theoretical Basis for Nursing, 5th Edition. Wolters Kluwer Health.

Simmons, Laurie. (2009). Dorthea Orem's Self Care Theory as Related To Nursing Practice in Hemodialysis. Nephrology Nursing Journal.

Watson, C. (2022). Overview of Pain. Merck Manuals. MerckManuals.com

Woo, T. (2019). Pharmacotherapeutics for Advanced Practice Nurse Prescribers Fifth Edition. F.A. Davis Company

More books at OASISNinja.com

Made in the USA
Las Vegas, NV
11 April 2024

88545964R10184